SECRETS & SHAME

JAMES W MERCER PH.D holds a Doctorate in
counseling psychology and a degree in funeral service. He
owns a foster care and adoption agency focusing on the
hundreds of children throughout Texas who have suffered
abuse. He lives in Austin with his partner and three
daughters and finds joy in his Jewish faith and community.

Follow James on Social Media:

🐦 @secretsandshame

📘 SecretsandShame

🌐 drjamesmercer.com

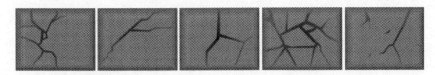

SECRETS & SHAME

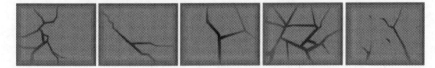

DEAR OPRAH DIARIES

James W. Mercer PH.D

ARCHWAY
PUBLISHING

Archway Publishing books may be ordered through booksellers or by contacting:

Archway Publishing
1663 Liberty Drive
Bloomington, IN 47403
www.archwaypublishing.com
1 (888) 242-5904

Because of the dynamic nature of the Internet, any web addresses or links contained in this book may have changed since publication and may no longer be valid. The views expressed in this work are solely those of the author and do not necessarily reflect the views of the publisher, and the publisher hereby disclaims any responsibility for them.

Any people depicted in stock imagery provided by Thinkstock are models, and such images are being used for illustrative purposes only. Certain stock imagery © Thinkstock.

ISBN: 978-1-4808-2988-6 (sc)
ISBN: 978-1-4808-2987-9 (hc)
ISBN: 978-1-4808-2986-2 (e)

Library of Congress Control Number: 2016906976

Print information available on the last page.

Archway Publishing rev. date: 6/30/2016

This book is dedicated to you, no matter the storm you're in, you are always able to find sunshine.

The Siamese Twins:
Secrets and Shame
My name is Secrets.
My Siamese twin is Shame.
We thrive in the dark.

Two of us are one.
We are inseparable.
Apart we will die.

We cause diseases.
We never rest nor retreat.
We will destroy you.

For breakfast we eat
Serenity and courage,
With a side of joy.

For lunch we devour
Peace salad with faith dressing.
Our dinner is light.

Our power is fear
That works amazingly well
To keep you in chains.

While you are asleep,
We fill your dreams with hatred,
Hatred of yourself.

This is quite a gig—
Unlimited volunteers,
Limitless secrets.

Trading Secrets and Shame for Serenity and Sanity

Telling my story,
Returning shame to senders,
Shame that was not mine.

Unveiling the truth,
Letting go of the outcome,
As healing begins.

Posting a large sign:
Rebuilding and Repairing,
No Destruction Zone.

Embracing with joy
Serenity/sanity,
Forgiveness and love.

Sharing my story
With those who are where I've been,
Giving others hope.

Prayers Answered in God's Time

Please send me true friends
To love me just like I am,
The way God made me.

Send me strong allies
Like my mother could not be,
More friends like Betsy.

Send me kind mentors,
Surrogate fathers to love
Who'll help me succeed.

Please send me a mate
To share life's joys and sorrows,
A true friend for life.

Help me be a dad,
Better than the one I had,
A father of girls.

Give me the courage
To tell my whole life story,
To start the healing.

The world is full of suffering. It is also full of overcoming it.

—Helen Keller

Prayers Answered in God's Time

Please send me true friends
To love me just like I am,
The way God made me.

Send me strong allies
Like my mother could not be,
More friends like Betsy.

Send me kind mentors,
Surrogate fathers to love
Who'll help me succeed.

Please send me a mate
To share life's joys and sorrows,
A true friend for life.

Help me be a dad,
Better than the one I had,
A father of girls.

Give me the courage
To tell my whole life story,
To start the healing.

The world is full of suffering. It is also full of overcoming it.
—Helen Keller

CONTENTS

CHAPTER 1

KILL THE MONSTER

I stood in the doorway holding the knife as the blood dripped down the blade, and the dark stains of my father's blood on my clothes began to stiffen. Euphoric in the knowledge that he would never hurt anyone again, my guts rebelled with the bile in my stomach and throat for what would come next. Having helped with a few hundred funerals, I knew what I had to do— clean up the mess and quick. I ran outside and grabbed the old tarp covering the moldering pile of wood we used for heat. I rushed back to the kitchen, where moments ago I had ended my torment and finally, *finally* rid us all of the monster.

Struggling, I rolled him over onto the outstretched tarp I had laid next to him on the floor. The air rushed from his lungs, filling the small room with the putrid smell of beer and cigarettes. I doubled over, trying not to puke right then and there from the smell. Slowly, I gained my composure and folded the tarp over him and rolled him once more, completing the cocoon that would forever hold all of my secrets and shame. I grabbed the frayed extension cord from under the sink and carefully tied up the package as best I could. Now for the hard part—digging a hole in the backyard like the many I had dug before to bury the stray cats that wandered in off the street, unaware that their deaths awaited from the monster who lived there. My eyes popped open. I was drenched in sweat. My first thought: *thank God this was just a dream.* My second thought: *damn, it was just a dream.*

I know the exact day I started plotting to kill Harry. On May 10, 1989, I wrote a note that said, "Kill him." The pencil I used to write those words pierced a hole into several pages in my Big Chief tablet because I stabbed them so hard into the paper.

It was near the end of my first year in elementary school and the day before my seventh birthday. I had wanted my mom to leave him and I had wanted to hurt him for a long time, but this was the day I decided my mom would never leave him. Somehow, some way, I would have to take things into my own hands.

If I had been aware—or perhaps I was—my hatred for him could have started when he found out my mom was pregnant with me and he left her, saying, "This is all your fault anyway. I told you the night I met you I never wanted no kids."

After Harry bolted, Uncle Jim and Aunt Rosie, who lived about six blocks away, took my mom into their home for a couple of months before and several weeks after I was born.

Uncle Jim and Uncle John, twins, were my mother's eldest siblings. She and her twin brother were the youngest of ten surviving kids in her family. My mom named me James after her favorite older brother (his twin, John, died in the Vietnam War) and gave me Wayne as my middle name after Harry, even though she didn't know where he was when I was born or whether he was ever coming back.

"When he ran out of money and couldn't con anyone else into giving him money," my aunt told me angrily several years later, "the bastard came home and took y'all back for your mom's disability check." Jim and Rosie had no children at that time.

Harry was my mother's first and only husband. Though only five feet, five inches tall, 135 pounds, he was as strong as a mule, especially when he was drunk. That, unfortunately for my mom and later for us kids, was most of the time. He had hazel-green eyes with a strange yellow ring in the middle.

His long, yellow, tobacco-stained teeth were falling out one by one, I now assume due to drug use but also probably because of the lack of dental hygiene and dental care that was either unavailable or unaffordable or that he outright rejected. He had thin lips that all but disappeared when he closed his mouth. His small ears protruded from his head.

Harry was very sensitive about a nose that was too large for his face. It had a large ball at the end, similar to a clown's nose. I'm sure he had been teased about it when he was young. I remember his decking more than one drunken companion who made fun of his nose. They usually only made that mistake once.

Forever etched in my memory—much like the smell of the first rotting cadaver I later encountered—is the stench of stale tobacco mixed with his favorite beer, Natural Light. Those are two smells I will never forget.

Whenever he talked, droplets of beer and spit would sail through the air and land on my food. If I had a plate near him, I never touched the food after his spit landed on it, no matter how hungry I was. And in those years, I was always hungry.

His right hand was stained yellow-orange where for years he had held his hand-rolled cigarettes filled with Bugler tobacco. He had an outline of the state of Texas tattooed on his right arm with *Texas* tattooed below it.

Harry was anything but religious, so it was confusing at first why he asked God to damn everything and why Harry thought God would even grant his lame request. The only time I ever heard him use God or Jesus' name, his favorite curse words, was during an angry tirade.

On the other hand, I have not one memory of Harry thanking God or Jesus for anything. He hated my mom's going to church on Sundays, accusing her of thinking she was better than everyone else and teaching us boys to be high and mighty.

"Also because," he would continue, "no one can be that happy about going to a goddamned fucking church full of hypocrites."

Anyway, by this time I had to be extremely cautious and accept the fact that the Big God just might be hiding in some invisible place above the earth, watching for the opportunity to answer Harry's prayer to damn me.

The only prayer Harry ever talked about praying was years later. After banishing me at age fifteen from the house and his life forever, he angrily told me he was praying that I would get AIDS and die. "Our family has been shamed and embarrassed enough by you," he'd rave on. "You'll get what you deserve one day."

Sometime long before I started kindergarten, I stopped referring to him as Dad or my dad, except when speaking or writing to figures of authority. I got the idea from my evil twin, Jamal. Jamal is not and never was an imaginary friend. In fact, he's not a friend at all. We are in a constant battle in my head, just like my brothers and I when we fought.

Jamal usually controls my first thought in every situation, but the good twin, James, tries his best to win out every time. I have to be honest and admit that Jamal does win on occasion no matter how hard I've tried to overrule him.

Jamal thought up and encouraged the secret act of rebellion of referring to Harry by his name. I instantly agreed with Jamal, and I decided that day that Shame and Rejection are the names of two-way streets in a very bad part of every small town.

From that time forward I would think of him as just Harry, or when I would rarely talk about him to my closest friends, I would refer to him as Harry. Harry was my unemotional word for him, but there was also a special way I had to say it. There was the slightest sound of disdain in my inflection but not the outright hate that was in my heart. I knew revealing that hate could have been met with a swift scolding by one of my Christian friends or retribution from any adult who might overhear.

Later in kindergarten I loved to hear a classmate, Carlotta, mimic my inflection of disdain. She could do it so much better than I, and we would laugh anytime she said, "How's Harry?" in our special code way.

We never really had much to do with my dad's siblings, even though they lived close to us when they weren't in jail for writing hot checks, public intoxication, prostitution, assault and battery, thievery, and other crimes too numerous to mention.

One of Harry's relatives threatened to kill a very well-known public figure and will be in prison for the rest of his life. Because Harry was the only one in his immediate family who never went to jail and/or prison that I ever knew of or heard anyone mention, he was the hero child in his family.

My mom is no bigger than a minute, reserved and shy. She rarely looks anyone in the eye and even then for only a second or two. Her head, full of long, auburn, wavy hair that smelled like Pert Plus she got free from the local thrift store, is held down most of the time like a whipped puppy.

Do not be fooled by her outward appearance, however. She may be five-foot-nothing tall, never more than ninety-five to a hundred pounds her whole life, even after a potluck on Sundays at church three or four times a year, but her heart is as big as all outdoors.

Her timid demeanor, coupled with the sweet nature and love that oozed from every pore, made everyone adore her. All the folks in our small town knew she had been and still was enduring unspeakable hardships, but no one knew what to do or how to help her.

At age eight, Mom was molested by a trusted family acquaintance, Mike. Mom reported the incident to her father, but he minimized it and never reported it. I'm sure he knew it might come out that he was also having sex with his own daughters. Later, after many more incidences with other little girls, Mike went to prison for his crimes and died several years later at the hands of inmates who had been molested as children.

Being the baby girl in a large family, my mom has no memory

of what life was like before her mom, Annie, died at age thirty-nine from breast cancer when Mom was seven years old. After her death, each daughter in succession was forced to become her dad's surrogate wife. At age sixteen, the eldest daughter, Melba Beth, ran away and moved in with her first cousin. They never married, but through the years they had four children, two in Special Ed.

My mom's dad was a bigger-than-life character. Only an inch over six feet tall, by the time I remember him he weighed 250 pounds. He slept in a cot under a tree in his yard the entire time I knew him. I loved my grandpa, and it was one of the great disillusionments of my adult life when I found out even as little as I did about his molestation of his daughters.

After Melba Beth left, Mom's second sister then was forced to serve as their dad's wife. She also ran away as a teenager. Mom was next in line and was forced into sexual servitude by her father at age eleven after her second sister ran away. Mom did not graduate high school because when she married Harry, she dropped out of school, like her sisters before her.

Often through the years Harry would torment Mom with innuendos and slurs about how much she had enjoyed having sex with her dad. He would say, "And you've been a whore ever since."

The accusations and punishment she would endure if she fixed herself up were too great to risk doing so. The only makeup she ever wore was foundation to cover the bruises on her face, and she only dared apply that after we got on the bus that picked us up for church on Sunday mornings.

More than once Harry accused her of having an affair with one of the drivers of the church bus. I had to admit to myself that even I had noticed the driver was a really handsome guy!

From a young age my mom verbally thanked a god for everything, so I knew there was a god, but I was not sure about the Big God—you know, the one who had made me the way I was. The one who had made me so defective that Harry and my schoolmates said vile things to and about me, long before I knew what they were talking about.

My mom suffered from seizures from the time she was a child. No one in the family knew, or could remember, when or why those seizures started, but they were traumatic for us kids to witness. She would start shaking uncontrollably all over, her eyes would roll back in her head, and we never knew if she would come out of one of them alive. In addition to the seizures, she was always recovering from bruises, broken bones, and headaches.

At occasional happy family get-togethers, my mom and her sisters loved to tell us kids the family oral history about our mother's mother Annie and Annie's mother Minnie, who were Jewish. We never tired of hearing that history. As the oral legend goes, my great-grandmother Minnie was born in Vienna, Austria, and escaped to America during the Holocaust. Her family settled in Chicago, Illinois, where she met Grandpa Clayton at a USO (United Service Organization) dance. He was in Chicago in the navy. They married, and he brought her back to Texas.

One of the great losses of Minnie's life was being unable to practice or share her religion because there was no synagogue in the small central Texas town where they settled. Grandpa Clayton was a strong Christian, and she just attended church with him to keep peace in the family.

She never stopped practicing her religion in a private way, keeping the high holy days and reciting the Hebrew blessings and singing the praises she had learned in her childhood.

From my earliest memories, Harry told me repeatedly he could not have been my dad because I was a sissy. After I absorbed the initial shock and anger at this contemptuous declaration, having no idea at the time what it actually meant except rejection, I decided that was fine with me because I didn't want him to be my dad any more than he wanted to be my dad.

My conscious hatred of Harry began long before I started school. I had a younger brother by that time named Adam, just less than two years younger than me. Everyone knew he was Harry's favorite because Harry loved to say, "Now that's my boy. He don't walk or talk like no sissy." Harry began repeatedly telling me I should be more like my brother: a masculine kind of boy who loved fighting and roughhousing and hated to take baths. That's when I first remember starting to plot ways to *hurt* Harry.

As soon as Harry would leave the house, going to some day job he picked up out of desperation to support his drinking, smoking, and drug habit before the next disability check arrived, Mom would push Adam in a used stroller as I walked alongside her several blocks away to the Love Center, where rich people left their used clothing for poor people to come try on and take home.

A sweet, grandmotherly person, known to the entire town as Aunt Taylor, ran the charity out of her converted garage as a volunteer for a local Catholic Church. Aunt Taylor had strange-looking hair. She slicked it back in front and on the sides into a flat ponytail. New growth stuck up above the slicked-back part and was gray, with yellow and green tints.

I'm sure now that's what the rich ladies covered up with a rinse that turned their hair blue, but Aunt Taylor was an old maid who had left the monastic community and her beloved convent to take care of her aging parents. She never wore makeup of any kind or did anything to change the way God made her.

I asked her on one visit what made her smell so good. She told me a dear friend in the church who was highly allergic to fragrances had donated boxes of sachet and perfumes left from when her grandmother had sold Avon back in the 1960s. The inventory of fragrances was found in her cedar chest after she died. Aunt Taylor said the supply had sold out immediately after it was donated. She even bought some herself. That night I made myself a note to remember when I got rich to buy Mom some sachet called *Somewhere*.

At the time I thought that was the most wonderful name I had ever heard and the most intoxicating smell I had ever smelled.

Somewhere sounded to me as a young child like a place where life was free of pain and suffering. Maybe that was because it was anywhere but *here,* where to me there was nothing *but* pain and suffering. The vision of the word *Somewhere* conjured up in my young mind was mainly any place far off where Harry was not.

When we found a shirt or pants we liked at the Love Center, we put it on either under or over the shirt or pants we were wearing. That way no one would ever know we took handouts. Taking handouts was a closely held secret in this small Texas town that meant you were poor, most likely prone to thievery, and certainly not to be trusted.

When Harry would find a sack of clothes under my bed from the Love Center, he would scoff, assuring us in both subtle and straightforward ways that rich people were not to be trusted. In fact, they were most likely the reason we were poor.

Harry would disgustedly explain, using meaningless anecdotal evidence, how the rich had selfishly grabbed too much of the proverbial pie, leaving us poor people with the crumbs they had either accidentally dropped or had magnanimously given to us to make themselves feel better. That was how Harry viewed all successful people.

Experience with my first real-life rich person, and many others after him, confirmed the fact that that was just another of Harry's many rationalizations for his failure to provide even the most basic necessities for his family.

After starting off my life at birth with Uncle Jim, I was always his favorite. He had wanted a son so badly, and for too short a time I became that son. He and Aunt Rosie even begged to adopt me when I was born because they could have provided so much better financially for my needs, but my mom would not let them do it. She said somehow, some way, our family would make it intact.

Uncle Jim, a gifted storyteller, took me everywhere he went when I was young, teaching me in what I now know was an attempt to steer me away from following Harry's example in the choices he was making. He taught me so much about business and life through running commentary, even though some of his stories were likely made up or at the very least embellished to make his points.

"There are more poor people than rich people," he loved to say when explaining how he was starting some new business catering to the masses. Uncle Jim always claimed to be broke but carried a large roll of cash in his right shirt pocket.

He was left-handed and had an invisible spring in his elbow that caused him to habitually check his right pocket with his left hand to confirm that the precious wad of hard-earned cash was still there.

Uncle Jim taught me at five years of age that any self-respecting man should carry plenty of cash with him. In the early years he was generous with me, never giving me money outright but always figuring out ways I could earn a little. His wife, Aunt Rosie, on the other hand, was a packrat and very tightfisted.

I learned early that Uncle Jim and I never discussed our business or financial transactions with Aunt Rosie. It would just worry her too much, I was told.

"There are always people needing cash," Uncle Jim would say. "If a friend asks you for a loan, ask him what he has that he can sell you. The more urgent his need, the less he will take for a valuable item. Always be kind, and remember that it takes a lot of courage for a man to ask another man for a loan.

"He don't have to make up some cockeyed, bullshit hard-luck story, and I don't even have to know or care why he needs the money. Maynard,"—that was his nickname for everyone—"you can make a good living buying and selling things while at the same time helping folks, and you don't need no college education for that neither," he would explain.

"When money leaves my pocket, I always get something more valuable than the cash to replace it. I don't have to threaten him, stalk him, or hurt him to be whole again. I am more than whole when I get him out of his bind.

"That way my friend—see there, he stays my friend—is relieved and happy, and I am happy because my net worth has just increased. Many times I have tripled my money in an hour or two, depending on the item. Any kind of farm equipment or guns costs me the least, goes the quickest, and brings me the most.

"Heck, let me reword that. He don't even have to be a friend. Sometimes I get a better deal from the strangers my friends refer to me. I guarantee you I could run for mayor and win the election in a landslide just because of all the people I've helped out of a financial bind.

"Now James, listen very carefully to what I'm about to tell you," Uncle Jim said seriously one day during the summer before I started kindergarten at age five. "Loaning money is one of the worst things you can do. Unless you own a bank one day, never loan nobody money.

"You might as well just give the person the money, rather than loan it. When you loan it, chances are very good you will never see it again anyway, and you will have missed the opportunity to experience the greater blessing of giving. Then you have not only lost your money but you've also lost a friend. I can't tell you how many families have busted up or killed one another over a ten-dollar loan."

I loved sharing my first name with this uncle, whom my mom and I both adored. Hating my middle name is one of my earliest memories. Looking back, I now know I really hated Harry, but hating his name was much safer.

Tumbleweed, Texas, is in the famous hill country right near the center of the state, not far from where President Johnson and President Bush had homes. There are beautiful rolling hills filled with wildflowers and native grasses.

People are friendly—some outsiders who come to town call us nosy—very generous, and extremely apologetic. One day I counted the number of times I heard someone say, "I'm sorry,

Bubba, it's all my fault," or "I'm sorry I bumped into you. That was my fault …"

I lost interest and stopped counting at sixty-seven. Those were the kinds of assignments Uncle Jim would give me to take my mind off of my home situation and to help me earn a little cash. When I would report back to him, he'd say, "Good job, Maynard. I needed that market research for a new business I'm considering buying. Now here's a dollar, but whatever you do, do not tell your dad where you got it or that you have it."

Another assignment Uncle Jim often gave me was to count the number of times someone said, "Bless your heart." It is so common that I didn't realize how often people said it until I was hired to count the times in one day. One of my teachers said it fifteen times in her fifty-minute class alone. It's a wonder there is any heart disease in Tumbleweed.

Uncle Jim would come to the house to get me, and my dad would be uncharacteristically kind and friendly to him (and me), saying, "James, your uncle is here to get you. Now you mind him and do whatever he says." My dad knew Uncle Jim always had a wad of cash, so Uncle Jim could do no wrong as far as my dad was concerned. I never heard a cross word spoken between them, although Uncle Jim made no secret of the fact that he hated the way my dad treated his sister and us kids.

Uncle Jim owned Rocking Horse Enterprises, a rock and limestone quarry, and from the age of eight I would write out his invoices for him each month because he liked my handwriting. I did that for several years. When he would pay me, he would tell me to get something for my mom and my brothers and me and not to tell Dad. I had to promise that not one penny of the money would go for anything for my dad.

Even though Uncle Jim neither gave me money nor loaned me money, I'm sure he would have gladly loaned me money (bought something from me) from time to time if I'd had something worth more that I could trade it for.

Like most folks, Uncle Jim's life was full of paradoxes. His business dealings to me were a confused combination of helping others and helping himself (and protecting himself from harm). I never really knew which trait was the most important to him. Luckily for him and all of the people he helped through the years, most of his dealings accomplished all three.

Chapter 2

Mounting Losses

Sometime before I was six and Adam was four, my mom had gotten pregnant again. She told me but no one else. She swore me to secrecy. We were so excited. Mom just knew this baby was a girl—the daughter she had always wanted. I was already a mom to my younger brother Adam, and I loved babies. I felt so proud I was the only person she told.

I began to design baby clothes out of scraps of cloth that my Aunt Rosie saved for me. Remembering those painful years, I realize I was already housewife, surrogate mom, cook, maid, clothes designer, fashion consultant, toilet shiner, and chief bottle washer at our house, although I never thought of it in those terms at the time. Now I was about to be a mom again! My joy filled the earth.

I noticed my mom was unusually lethargic. She did not want to get out of bed. She was nauseated and vomited nonstop, day after day. She was probably about three months along, but because her body was so tiny, she was already beginning to show.

Long before daylight one morning, loud voices woke me up, and I raced to the cracked door of my mom's room. Harry could not find his camouflage hunting pants and shirt. He jerked Mom out of bed and angrily pushed her toward the closet to find them before his buddy arrived to pick him up.

Mom sleepily stumbled in the dark over a pair of his boots he had laid out for his hunting trip. She tripped, and fell face first into the messily laid out pile of his shotgun, boxes of shells and hunting gear directly onto her rounding belly. She grasped her belly with screams of pain.

She went into a seizure. Harry's ride arrived and honked loudly, and he said, as he skipped and hopped toward the front door, putting on his boots one at a time and almost knocking me off my feet, "Oops, Jimbo's here. You take care of the bitch. She's probably just faking anyway. It'll pass. It always does. I gotta go."

There are no words to describe the fear and anger that gripped me that day. Mom's eyes were rolled back in her head, her nose was bleeding from the fall, and there was a large puddle of blood underneath her hips when I turned her over onto her back. She whispered for me to quickly get her a towel and firmly ordered me back to bed. After the loss of my much-anticipated baby sister at the hands of the monster who called himself a husband, I was always terrified to leave my mom alone with Harry.

I now know that there is a psychological phenomenon called witness abuse. One of the hardest situations I endured as a child was watching Harry terrorize my mother or brothers.

When Harry would begin beating my mother or one of my brothers for some real or imagined infraction, I'd immediately say something like, "No, Dad! Stop beating Mom. Look over here at me. I'm the one you are angry with. I'm your sissy son, remember?"

Anger strong enough to kill would then overcome Harry, and he would instantly pivot and start in on me. No matter how hard the beating, I was always relieved that my mom or brothers were saved from that horribly painful fate.

The beatings got out of hand one Sunday. I went in to my mom and Harry's room to ask my mom if my new secondhand outfit from the Love Center was okay for church. I was standing there in socks and shorts, holding up my shirt, pants, and tie in front of me for Mom's advice. Harry made the mistake of hitting me really hard in the face, rearranging my nose and blackening my eyes.

He was convinced I wanted to have sex with my mom, and he went into great, repulsive detail about what I was fantasizing doing with her. He totally went off the rails. Looking back, he probably should have been admitted to a treatment center — or better yet, taken to jail because of the danger he was to all of us.

For probably two months before, during, and after my mom's pregnancy and miscarriage, my brothers and I essentially had no mom. She was sick with headaches, depressed, or sleeping most of the time. The rest of the time we would hear her softly sobbing to herself. Harry uncharacteristically did not scold her for what he would ordinarily call her laziness during this time. He just, happily for us, stayed away from home for days at a time.

Several times a year in the early years, Harry would disappear for days at a time with no food in the house and no parting explanation. When Mom's disability check would arrive, he would come back around, buy limited staples, get Mom pregnant if she weren't already pregnant, and then leave again, talking really fast about some fabulous out-of-town job waiting for him.

He would promise lots of food, toys, and books when he got paid and returned. He made ridiculous notes of our wish lists, behaving as though he was a contender for the father of the year award.

At the time I did not know he had no job and no money except my mom's disability income check he cashed and took with him for what he always called "my travel expenses." When he became angry with me, he would threaten to take away his fictitious "military check" that he claimed supported us all.

My mom later apologetically admitted to me she allowed us boys to believe this lie. She wanted us to think he was the breadwinner in the family as a good example to us boys and so

Harry would feel like the man of the house. At the time she told me she hoped just maybe he would be nicer to us.

When he would decide for any number of reasons to leave us, he would promise his undying love to my sleeping mom's limp, lifeless form that barely showed her bed was unmade. As bad as I hated him, when he would leave I was stricken with fear about how we would survive.

Because we had a house, we were not homeless, he would often tell us. Not once did he acknowledge the fact we were often food*less*, except on the occasions when he would explain that the reason we had no food left was because we kids ate like pigs at a trough when we did have food.

My brothers and I loved the times when Harry would be away from home and we could play and laugh and scream at the tops of our lungs. The household was totally different during those far-too-few treasured moments.

Guilt and shame over her forced sexual affair with her father, fear of her husband's alcoholism and brutality, fear of the seizures that had beset her since childhood, and repressed anger over her victim state all were like a lid on a pressure cooker that held in a happy-go-lucky seven-year-old girl who had never been able to even find out who she was or why she had been born.

Occasionally circumstances, such as Harry's being away from home, allowed the tightly sealed lid on her natural personality to cautiously lift, and out would effervesce that fun-loving seven-year-old girl trapped inside of her. That most likely was the girl her siblings knew and loved before their mother died. How we cherished those moments of carefree fun that are some of the most vividly happy memories of our childhood.

So often bruised and hurting physically from Harry's violent attacks against her, Mom would ignore her pain and pretend to be the perfect Igor, hunching over like she was about to pick something up, then throwing her weight from left to right, intermittently dragging her limp arms and then clenching them like claws, thrusting them toward us with the most evil look on her face and with threatening guttural sounds coming from deep within her chest.

The chase would ensue, with her stalking us around the house, hiding and seeking, making scary noises, and tickling us to hysteria when she would catch up with us or trap us. When Mom's pain from her headaches, bruises, sprains, or broken bones that were the consequence of Harry's repetitive abuse would get to be too much during our playtime, she would walk over to the couch and pretend to be a dead body while she rested.

I would do her hair and makeup, place her hands across one another on her chest, and place a wildflower from the yard between her fingers, and we would eulogize her right there. I could never use mascara to make up her eyes because if any traces remained when Dad returned, he would accuse her of having an affair.

Adam would be the minister, I was the funeral director, and Joseph would dramatically take on the role of a mourner. It was so hard to remain somber when Joseph would switch into mourning mode, crying loudly with fake tears, throwing himself over Mom's body, and then looking up with a serious look on his face to see if anyone was watching, momentarily forgetting his act. Every time in mere seconds we all—including Mom, the deceased—would immediately break out in raucous, deep belly laughter.

I have often asked myself if those happy childhood memories would have been that much fun if we hadn't suffered so much mental, physical, and emotional trauma at the hands of our hated predator. Ironically, our happiest play revolved around our gentle mom pretending to be a monster chasing us, followed by all of us participating in tableaux depicting her death.

In a single afternoon with Mom, we would instantly go from the depths of despair to the heights of elation as soon as Harry's ride would back out of the driveway, taking him safely away from us.

These times were too often cut short by a car pulling back into the driveway, crunching over the loose gravel, returning the monster to his castle. That was our daily alarm. Each of us instantly and automatically returned to quiet mode without a word being spoken.

On the first day of kindergarten, I met three new friends: Carlotta, Nancy, and Betsy. Betsy did everything she could to distract me from the intractable fear and sorrow that weighed me down the minute my mom left me at school. It was true I was sad for my mom to leave, but more than that, I was afraid of what Harry would do to her while I was gone.

In addition, I was still grieving for my dead sister from the year before. In an attempt to comfort me, one day Betsy came to school with a sack that contained a pink Care Bear with a rainbow across its tummy.

Everything about that Care Bear was symbolic but also prophetic. I slept with that bear until its tragic end at the hands of a real-life monster.

What I do remember vividly is grieving the loss of my sister with no one to tell but Nancy or Carlotta or Betsy at school. I had held in my grief for almost a year, only crying to myself at night and to Betsy when she would let me.

She finally got annoyed with me for not getting over the incident, so I turned to Nancy, who had infinite patience with me. Every chance we got that fall we'd sit on the playground while I poured out my heart to her during recess or briefly after school before we raced home like jumped rabbits, knowing we'd be in serious trouble for being late.

This daily ritual continued off and on for weeks. I also clearly remember the moment less than a year later that, without notice, I was through actively grieving. My seemingly bottomless well of tears and sadness was one day happily drained dry when my second brother, Joseph, was born in February of 1989, two months before I turned seven.

Joseph was a beautiful, tiny baby with bright blue eyes and blond hair. I fell in love with him instantly and whispered to him on many occasions how sorry I was he had to be born into this family. I promised him I would do everything in my power to protect him from the monster my mom had married.

Until the tragically premature death of my unborn sister, I only wanted to hurt Harry for what he was doing and saying to me. After that, I began plotting how to kill him for doing what he did to my mom, my miscarried sister, and my brother.

As the back-to-back losses in my life during those first years in kindergarten and the first grade were coming to a critical point, I began making a list of ways and reasons to kill Harry. Next on my list of reasons was added after Betsy gave me the Care Bear. Aunt Taylor at the Love Connection had the most beautiful baby doll I had ever seen.

Looking back, the feelings that doll brought out in me were indicative of my deep desire to be a parent from the earliest age. I would say it was my desire to be a dad, but I think my innate desire was really much more maternal.

That doll's bright blue eyes opened and shut, and I was instantly in love with her. I lied and told my mom and Aunt Taylor I needed it to give to Betsy for her birthday. I took it home and played for hours with that doll under my sweat pants, pretending I was pregnant.

I loved, nurtured, nursed, and confided in that doll until Harry found her in my room, along with a pair of Mom's beautiful high heels from the Love Connection, and my beloved doll was my first encounter with cremation. Harry made me watch him throw her and Mom's beautiful high heels onto a pile of burning trash, and as I watched her burn, something inside of me died that day as well. My grief was almost unbearable. Later that week my friend Nancy and her big brother helped me write this poem as a promise to myself:

> Good-bye, sweet Beth.
> Your wrongful death
> Will be avenged
> Before my last breath.

I had plotted from my earliest childhood memory how to *hurt* Harry for the things he was doing to me, but after witnessing the cremation, hurting him was no longer enough.

I then began having a hard time concentrating on anything but how to *kill* Harry and to rid the world of him once and for all. My friend Carlotta provided the first clue on how I might do it without getting killed myself instead—or even worse to me at the time, getting caught.

Since the first time I met her, she told me almost every day, "I love my grandmother more than anyone in the whole world." Carlotta came to school the day after the cremation I had just witnessed, seriously upset because her beloved grandmother had had to go to the hospital after taking too much Ex-lax, an over-the-counter chocolate-flavored disc used as a remedy for constipation back in those days.

I overheard Carlotta's mom telling my mom at the grocery store that her mother had become seriously dehydrated before telling anyone she was constipated or that she was taking the laxative. Instead of a simple bout of constipation, she had a bowel blockage, and for days she was not expected to live.

My Aunt Rosie always had a large package of Ex-lax discs in her bathroom. This is my first memory of sneaking into someone's house and stealing something that was not mine. As I opened the back door, I could see Aunt Rosie sleeping on the couch in front of her black-and-white television tuned loudly to *As the World Turns*, her favorite soap opera. My heart was beating out of my chest as I raced home with my stolen makeshift weapon.

Almost immediately I started spiking Harry's food with Ex-lax. Each time he started drinking alcohol, he entered a merry phase after consuming one to two and a half beers when he loved everyone and everything—even cats! When that phase quickly morphed into his angry phase as he gulped more beer, I would surreptitiously spike some food and take him the first warm serving in an uncharacteristically cheerful and loving manner.

I had plan A and plan B. Plan A turned out to be just another fantasy. I was hoping that maybe the diarrhea would start soon, he would decide it was the beer, give it up, and become a loving husband and father. When plan A didn't work, I went to plan B which, I sadly learned, was also fraught with problems.

During arduous trial and error, I soon discovered that my Ex-lax plan included too mild a dose. It took too long to take effect. And when it finally worked, Harry would accuse my mom of trying to poison him, always blaming the food I had surreptitiously spiked with Ex-lax. To this day he will not eat brownies of any kind—especially ones fresh out of the oven.

I considered a knife as a means of dispatching Harry for only a few seconds. That would mean I would have to get too close to him, inhaling the acrid combined odor of cheap beer, body odor strong enough to make me gag, and stale cigarette smoke. That was not going to happen.

Smothering him with a pillow while he was in a drunken stupor was something I considered more than once. However, even though he was a small man, I knew he could have easily overpowered me and killed me instead or called in one of his powerful friends to do it for him. When he was disturbed or abruptly awakened while sleeping off a bender, his anger-fueled strength was superhuman.

I've often thought how thankful I am that many years passed before I read about a distraught abused wife who set fire to her inebriated husband's bed.

When school was almost out for the summer in 1989, completely at my wits' end from the relentless chaos, beatings, and stress of trying to protect mom and my brothers as well as myself, I went to the post office and bought a postcard. I wrote my mom's sister, Aunt Luann, and asked her to come get us so we could go to her house for a visit. I always included a postscript at the bottom of any card I sent her, begging her not to tell my mom or dad I'd written her or I'd be in big trouble.

Uncle Eugene and Aunt Luann were packrats who never cleaned their house. My first day of every visit I would straighten up, sweep, mop, clean the toilet, and dust so we could stand to be there. I did not want my brothers or me to catch any bad diseases.

That's the first time I saw a porn magazine. Uncle Eugene had heterosexual porn, homosexual porn, and all sorts of weird porn magazines. Down in the stack of regular magazines, stuck deep inside the pages of a farm equipment catalogue I held up by the spine and shook to clear off the dust, were several folded and smeared mimeographed pages of hand-drawn, cartoon-like cowboy characters, naked except for boots, spurs, and ten-gallon hats and with their pants down around their ankles, having sex with different animals.

The men's erect penises were huge. I remember wondering how those guys ever sat down, much less rode a horse, without breaking it off. For a second or two, before catching myself, I laughed out loud uncontrollably at the funny looks drawn on the animals' faces.

Afraid of getting caught by waking up Uncle Eugene with my laughter, I quickly shoved everything under the seat cushion of the couch except a John Deere catalogue. I started casually perusing the catalogue, lightly licking the middle finger of my right hand and slowly turning each page like I had once seen a rich woman do when reading her Bible in church—my heart beating out of my chest until I was absolutely convinced Uncle Eugene was still snoring.

Since our uncle slept during the day and would rage at us if we made the slightest sound, we would go outside and play in the acreage around their house while he slept.

We dug holes with Uncle Eugene's empty snuff cans, old broken spoons, or anything we could find that would break the ground. We let our imaginations soar. Once we were sure we were getting very close to China in our digging.

On more than one occasion, we had a rare meeting of our

minds and stopped digging. We were afraid a starving Chinaman could pop out of the hole. We would have to share our limited food with him, and we could not communicate with him. Uncle Eugene had made it clear he wanted no visitors other than family, and we had enough problems without asking for another "whoopin'."

My brothers and I loved to climb trees and be King of the World from the highest branch. Because I was the eldest, the moniker King of the World (KOTW) usually was bestowed on me, by me. My younger brothers were afraid to climb as high as I would, so the height and the status that came with it meant I was it.

Uncle Eugene always had a stack of used cardboard boxes out back near their chicken coop. After we finished with the chore of scooping up chicken droppings, we made houses, pulpits, doghouses, and forts out of the boxes. That was hot, dusty work, but there was a water sprinkler that we could turn on for our bath before we could come in the house for supper. What a treat and respite from the hot Texas sun that warm water would be when we'd all be covered in dirt and the putrid smell of the chicken droppings.

Since I was the eldest sibling, I was the teacher. My two younger brothers at the time were the students. Adam, the brother nearest me, was a whiz in math. He did not appreciate it when I would correct him during our play because he was always better at math than I was. A scuffle would almost always break out while we were playing school. We spent a lot of time during the summers bloodying each other's noses and patching each other up, only to start afresh the next day.

Their three-bedroom, one-bath mobile home was high above the ground on pier and beam, so we spent many hours under the house, out of the hot Texas sun, exploring all the critters that lived under there. We were stung several times but were never seriously injured.

My brothers and I would dig shallow holes and see who could pull the fattest, longest worm or strangest critter out of the ground.

Every activity was a life-and-death competition. I almost always won that contest, according to me, so when I would declare that indisputable fact, a fight would predictably break out. There was no contest the day I pulled the longest, fattest, albino worm out of the ground. Everyone agreed, for the first time without a fight, that I was the hands-down winner that day.

One day after a busy Saturday in town buying groceries and supplies, we crawled back under the house and were delighted to find a mother dog and eleven puppies! She only had ten teats, so it became my job to see that the runt got his turn at the dinner table. I would go under the house several times a day, pull one of the fattest puppies away, squealing and screaming, and quickly replace it with the runt.

Aunt Luann, bless her heart, interceded and persuaded Uncle Eugene to keep the runt—eventually finding homes for all the others—and that puppy became my best friend, my confidant and sidekick. I begged Harry to let me take him home, but he cursed, "No, goddammit! I ain't being woke up by some bastard barking dog!"

That was the first time in the two weeks I had been gone that I had had one thought about killing Harry. That two-week respite from hatred had been so refreshing.

Each summer I grieved as I said good-bye to the runt named Amigo, who was secretly Ami to me. One of my and Ami's deep, dark secrets was that the reason he was so small and the odd man out in his litter was because he was really a female pup trapped in a male pup's body.

When Uncle Eugene and Aunt Luann were getting ready to take us home on Uncle Eugene's day off, which was Thursday, June 29, a friend of Uncle Eugene's at his work who had a yearly fireworks stand for the holiday, brought by a box of fireworks for us kids to have to celebrate the Fourth of July out in the country.

I overheard Uncle Eugene firmly state when handing him a stack of magazines in return, "Now I'm only loaning you these trade magazines so you can buy yourself a new tractor (wink, wink). I will need them back as soon as possible."

We spent endless excited hours reading the labels of the boxes of fireworks, imagining what they would look like as we lit them and watched them sail into the sky before bursting into a spectacular display of sound and light. Adam and I had never seen fireworks.

Since Adam was Dad's favorite, I carefully primed him on how to beg Harry to let us stay until after the Fourth of July. Harry said absolutely not; I had to get home and help my mother with four-month-old baby Joseph and all the work around the house because he was leaving on a big job out of town. We returned home reluctantly and sadly as scheduled on Thursday.

After we got home, just the sight of Harry nauseated me. I could not eat. I went straight to bed. The next morning Harry jerked me out of bed by one arm and called me a "lazy, no-good-for-nothing, pouting faggot" while beating me with his belt across my buttocks. The more I resisted, the harder he hit me.

I was dancing around, kicking my feet high in the air, trying to avoid the blows, when he hit me full force between my legs from behind squarely on my genitals with a plastic belt. I passed out. I have no idea how long I lay there. Luckily for both of us, when I woke up Harry was nowhere to be found for several days.

The following day my brother Adam fell off a low tree limb and badly scraped his knee. My mom took a dime from a pouch she had hidden and sent me to the store for alcohol. While there I ran into my friend Nancy and her mother, and they invited me to go with them the next morning to a local Baptist church. Nancy explained it was the first day of Vacation Bible School, that there was a going to be a big potluck luncheon, and her uncle drove the church bus that would come and pick us up.

We were out of food at home. I walked home as fast as I could, still swollen and in pain between my legs, to tell my mom. She agreed we should all go to church while Harry was gone.

My mom had always loved to tell us kids Bible stories from the Old Testament. She taught us all to pray, and I knew how much she loved her god. I was skeptical, thinking that if her god were anything like Harry, she could keep him. After she named me for her favorite brother and a Bible character, she subsequently picked out my two younger brothers' names also to honor Bible characters.

I loved Vacation Bible School. My teacher was named Mr. Boles. Everyone called him Brother, but I was too literal and uncomfortable using that word in referring to him, not knowing what it meant or why they called him that. He was also the Sunday school teacher during the school year.

All the mothers and teachers made cookies for our snack break each morning, and that was the first time I had ever tasted homemade lemonade. Homemade lemonade on a hot Texas summer day is something everyone should experience in his or her lifetime. I was convinced it was nectar straight from a funnel in the Big God's hands to my mouth. I was also convinced it would have been impossible for some small god to grow those wonderful lemons and sugar cane and send the rain to fill the wells with that wonderful water. Nope, I concluded, that was the job only my mom's Big God could have accomplished.

From those years in church, I remember well the stories of Adam and Eve, Cain and Abel, Noah and the Ark, and Moses bringing the Ten Commandments down from the mountain. I remember in Sunday school one day loudly defending Cain for killing his younger brother Abel.

"Duh, because God liked Abel better," I answered when my clueless, ordinarily brilliant friend, Hector, who was an only child, argued with the teacher. The teacher immediately tried to point out the grave error in my thinking, but I knew, having other brothers who were favored, there was absolutely no question that I was right about that argument.

However, not once, no matter how mad I got, did I ever think of killing any of my brothers, even though Harry made it clear he liked them better. Maybe I thankfully had too much blood, sweat, and tears invested in them by the time they got old enough to make me mad.

It was true that my brothers were the source of some of my greatest childhood sadness and anger, but they were also active participants in some of my greatest joys and fondest memories—because of our shared history and suffering, I later decided. As I wrote an essay in English class about Vacation Bible School, I felt a renewed gratitude that murdering, or even thinking of murdering a brother, was one sin I had completely dodged.

Chapter 3

Fostering Care

The suicidal thoughts first started when a policeman and ambulance were called to the house one Saturday night after a fight broke out over a game of dominoes. Sambo was a mentally challenged young man who was a math savant. He never went to school, but he was the best domino player of all of Harry's friends. Harry always wanted him for a partner.

Sambo knew after everyone played the first round what dominoes everyone most likely had left in his hand. After several hours of drinking beer that night, Luther, Harry's partner, got tired of Sambo winning every hand, and he angrily accused Sambo and his partner, Ray, of cheating. Sambo was tongue-tied and hard to understand, but calling him a cheater was fighting words, and everyone understood without asking for clarification every single word in a long stream of curse words that came out of his mouth that night.

Sambo picked up the edge of the card table in the backyard and threw dominoes, beer, and change flying toward Luther. He hit him in the belly with the edge of the table, pushing him, chair and all, over backward while flipping the table upside down on top of Luther. Sambo jumped up and down on the bottom of the table, as angry as I had ever seen anyone.

Luther weighed over three hundred pounds, but he was no match physically for the much younger Sambo, who was tall, skinny, wiry, and tough as a mule—especially when he was mad. Ray and Harry were going at each other a few feet away, fists flying, when Sambo started screaming.

He had picked the table up off of Luther, who was knocked out cold, blood pouring from his nose. All attempts to revive him were in vain. Everyone sobered up immediately. I ran to the neighbors' house and told them to call an ambulance. In two or three minutes an ambulance, fire truck, and police car came screaming up to the house, lights and sirens blaring.

Harry had warned us repeatedly to be deathly afraid of the police and black people. There are no words to explain the fear that gripped us that night when we had to deal with both of those eventualities directly for the first time in our lives. Worse yet, one of the policemen was also black!

Sambo was handcuffed and put in the back of the squad car, and Luther was loaded into the ambulance. Adam was about three, and I was between four and five. There was no food in the house. Adam and I were in the back corner of the yard, huddled together and crying in fear. One of the policemen came toward us, picked up Adam and me in each arm, and took us to the patrol car.

He loaded us in the backseat with Sambo, who kept screaming at us with his pronounced nasal lisp to shut up. Adam and I both sat in the police car, screaming anyway, until a black man drove up in a car. The policeman talked with him for a few minutes while Adam and I were screaming loudly, trying to tell the officer I had to go back inside and take care of my mama.

Adam was crying and clinging to me with what seemed like a death grip. I calmed down, trying to calm Adam down. I screamed to the policeman with all my might, "My mama's gonna die if I don't get back to her." The policeman ignored my pleas, picked us both up together in his arms, and put us in the back of the unknown black man's car. The policeman's calm demeanor and low, deep voice soothed our nerves.

Very late in the night we arrived at Mrs. Lambert's emergency foster home to spend the night. Adam and I were both hysterical. Mrs. Lambert, a black, kind, sweet widowed grandmother, had two other foster kids she was taking care of as well. Our screaming woke those kids up, and Mrs. Lambert kept talking very low so I would have to stop crying to understand what she was saying.

Her voice was soft and gentle as she calmly said, "Let me warm you kids up some supper. I bet you are both hungry after your busy night." Without waiting for a response that wasn't coming anyway, she went to the refrigerator and got out some greens, ham hock, potato salad, beans, and cornbread. She started warming everything up on the stove, and we ate every bite of the food she gave us. We were both starving. I even ate some beans, and I hated beans. I still do, but not that night.

Adam was sitting in my lap facing me with his face buried in my chest sobbing until the plates of warm food were set on the table. He turned around, smelled and saw the good food, and stopped crying. By the time we were full, Adam turned back around, falling asleep onto my chest.

Mrs. Lambert led us to a room with an empty lower bunk bed and told us just to rest for a while until she could find out what was happening. Her voice was so kind and reassuring, not anything like Harry had taught us to expect from all black people—and just the opposite of Harry!

Adam lay on top of me on the bottom bunk as Mrs. Lambert pulled a quilt made of airplane patches over us. Under those airplanes I felt a strange sense of calm and safety. While going to sleep that night, I pretended I was my Uncle John flying an airplane before he got killed in the war.

Mrs. Lambert said a prayer over us while she pointed to the four corners of our bed.

Five little angels 'round my bed,
One at the foot, one at the head,
One to watch, one to pray,
And one to take my sins away.

That's all I remember until I woke up the next morning to the smell of frying bacon and eggs and scratch biscuits baking in the oven. Adam and I both slept all night with no one to worry about but each other. We were together, holding on to each other all night with all our might.

A part of me wanted us to stay with Mrs. Lambert forever, but another part of me knew I couldn't stay there with my belly full while my mother and brother were hungry and in danger at home without me.

I have no idea how long we stayed with her, but I knew I had to do anything to get back to my mama. I started screaming, cursing, and kicking at her. I wouldn't do anything she asked me to do. I secretly coached Adam to start acting mean and hateful too so we could go home. I started coaching him too late.

He was already calling her, "Mama," and he kept crawling up in her lap and going to sleep while she rocked him in a rocker where she sat most of the time when she wasn't up cooking or cleaning. I was furious with him. Stupid kid. *He* never *does one thing I say,* I thought to myself.

A lady with bright red hair came to get me one morning, and I thought she was going to take us both home. I started kicking and screaming when she took me—but left my brother! That was the first time I had been away from him since he had been born. He had slept with me since he was a newborn, and a part of me was lost without him. But another part was also secretly relieved that he would have food to eat and a kind woman to stay with—a kind woman he already loved.

After Mrs. Lamberts house, I was taken to the home of an old, retired school teacher with black and white chin hairs who told me I was not going to get away with acting ugly in her house, so I could just do it the easy way or the hard way. "The choice is yours," she said firmly. I decided the easy way might be better because by that time I was just too exhausted to fight her. I went into a shell and never said one more word while I was at her house.

I grieved silently over my mom and brother until the pain reached an unbearable level. A night or two later after the house was quiet, I tiptoed into the kitchen to find some poison under her sink to drink and kill myself. Her cabinets were tied shut. I tiptoed back to the bedroom, disappointed, and sobbed myself to sleep, worried sick about my mama. At least I knew my brother was doing fine.

Adam and I were taken home in a few days. There was a lot of food in the cupboards—more than I had ever seen in my life. Harry acted so glad to see us—hugging us and telling us how much he loved us and had missed us. I stood there stiff as a board. I was holding my breath so I didn't have to smell him, much less confirm the ridiculous ruse he was perpetrating on the naïve transporter. Adam clung to the side of my legs with his head turned backward where he could not see Harry.

Harry apologized to the lady who took us home, swearing it was just a misunderstanding that had never happened before and certainly would never happen again. He blamed everything on his stupid friends. He even offered to make her a cup of coffee, and my mom and he didn't even drink coffee. I don't know what he would have done if she had said she wanted a cup.

Child Protective Services came to the school on several occasions to talk to me about bruises and sprains and broken bones, but I never let on that anything was wrong at home. Everything had always happened in some bizarre accident I fabricated right on the spot.

Dear Oprah:

My friend did a bad thing at school and had to go to the principal. When he got to his office, the police were there and took him away. They took him to a coach's house, who tried to make him play ball. He hated every minute of it. The coach was as tall as the jolly green giant, and my friend was way too short. He could not even throw the ball hard enough to hit the net on the basket. His wife was nice though, and when my friend started helping her clean house, they asked him if he wanted to come live with them. They had a big house and lots of food, and my friend wanted to stay there because nobody was drunk or cussed him out, but he had to go home and take care of his mama, who was sick and his brothers. Anyway, one good thing was that the coach never called him a sissy and never told him he was throwing a ball like a girl. I ain't writing down my friend's name cause he says it's a family secret and he don't want no one to ever find out he was taken away from his mama, and I know you wouldn't tell nobody.

Do you know why coaches always want their kids to play ball when they don't want to? Somebody needs to talk to coaches 'bout that. Maybe you could help a lot of people and have a show on that.

Sincerely,
James, your friend and fan in Tumbleweed, Texas

I've thought of Mrs. Lambert frequently through the years. I wanted badly to go back to her house many times for some more of her good cooking and to apologize for the way I had treated her. I wanted to take my mom and brothers with me, but I didn't want to hurt my mom's feelings because she might think I thought she was a better cook than my mama. That wasn't true. Mrs. Lambert just had good food to cook. Also, food just always tastes better when I'm really hungry.

I don't know how I remembered the prayer she prayed over me, but I prayed that prayer with Adam each night—with one major change. Adam and I were way more afraid of monsters than sin—in fact, we weren't afraid of sin at all—so we changed the last line to, "And one to keep the monsters away." One monster was what we were really afraid of in those early years. I always gave that fifth angel full credit when Harry was too drunk at night to bother us while we slept.

CHAPTER 4

A SAFE HIDING PLACE

E very child needs a safe hiding place. I now know that it is no accident that mine was in a tiny bedroom closet in my and my brothers' room where we all slept together. Weeds may have been visible coming up through the dried, rotting, and curling-up wooden bedroom floors, but as soon as I closed the door, there were no lies, no cursing, no angry rants, and everyone and everything was perfect. I was a hand in a warm glove, a turtle in my protective shell.

I had a large stack of carefully folded clothes on the bare floor in the back of that closet that hid a place I had cut out of the sheetrock with a rusty kitchen knife, covering the wall behind the hanging clothes.

Behind that piece of sheetrock was a two-by-four wooden cross plate that held a journal Aunt Rosie got from her insurance man each year that she never used, and I took a prior year's from her desk. Inside the notebook I placed a picture of me at six years old that I also found in her desk to use as a bookmark.

That hole in the wall in that warm, safe closet also became the safe haven where I hid many treasures throughout the years—each time carefully putting the piece of sheetrock back in its place and returning the stack of clothes in front of it to hide my treasures from the monster who lived in that house.

Lots of kids have an invisible friend. My friend, that treasured journal, was a tangible, perfect one—always there, always available, never angry, and yes, always willing to help me add another chapter to a book I would one day work up the courage to write.

Through the years when I was in my closet, perfect was the operative word. My mother was perfect—already having realized her dream since childhood of becoming a nurse. She had only wanted one child so she could pursue that dream. That's why my fabricated fantasy mother was already an award-winning, accomplished nurse, always helping heal those who were sick and hurting. In my childish way, I was helping my mom fulfill her dream.

My dad was also perfect. My favorite made-up memories were of our imaginary fishing trips together—the kind where guys are just hanging out without saying a word but silently and lovingly supporting one another. Also, it was clear to me as an observer that they were somehow invisibly and mysteriously bonding while creating lifelong memories.

Those were the stories of perfect families I first heard shared at funerals when a beloved parent or grandparent would die. Those stolen stories soon became my own story to anyone who would listen to me.

Instead of imaginary friends, I survived either on creating imaginary close relationships with live people—or my favorite— creating fantasy characters to help me survive my abuse. For instance, I could go into great detail on Monday mornings at school, regaling my classmates with stories about our fabulous father/son activities after a particularly brutal and chaotic weekend.

Those stories always involved falling on rocks on the bank of the river, getting a lure caught somewhere in my body, or some other bizarre accident that would explain the bruises and scratches and scabs on my body. I loved to recreate the falls or accidents physically, making my audience laugh hysterically and to forget any questions they might have about any possible parental abuse.

As I got older, my fantasy life in my closet involved two possible fathers who would be proud to claim me as a son: fathers I could love and not hate, fathers I would never have to plot how to kill, fathers who would love me back just the way I was.

My favorite time for creating these fathers was during the time I was keeping myself awake at night waiting for everyone to go to sleep so I could then check and make sure my mom and brothers were safely asleep.

The next favorite time was when I would first begin to regain consciousness in the morning, before completely waking up or opening my eyes. I would get furious during those times when I would be interrupted by a brother saying, "Are you awake or asleep, Bubba?" The magical spell would then always be broken, crashing me back to dreaded reality.

I wrote a letter to my first real father, a famous, fabulous, flamboyant, bodacious, rich gay dancer in Las Vegas, Nevada. He/she had many friends who were movie stars, producers, and directors.

At age seven to nine, I was too young and innocent to be concerned with the fact of how his sperm ended up in my mother's uterus, creating me. That was totally immaterial at the time.

Why would I worry about that when I tried not to be curious or even think about how I was conceived in the first place? I now know I was afraid I might learn the answer to that scary question.

Here is my first letter. Carlotta and her big brother helped me look up all the big words.

My dear fabulous, famous, flamboyant, bodacious, rich Las Vegas entertainer:

This letter may be a shock to you, but I hope you will let me call you Dad. You probably never wanted children, but I truly believe you are my real father. My mother's bastard husband says I am a bastard 'cause he would never have had a sissy son. If you can send me a bus ticket to Las Vegas, I will fix your hair, makeup, nails, and clothes where you will be more beautiful than any girl dancer on the Las Vegas strip. Even if we learn we are not father and son, I know we will love and support each other just the way we are, and you will never look more fabulous than when I finish your makeover. After that, we will be dear friends for life, and I'm sure I can prove to you that our relationship would be more valuable than the cost of a bus ticket.

Praying you are my real father,
James, Tumbleweed, Texas

P.S. Also, please consider the fact that if you are my real father, or if our friendship is as fun and happy as I know it will be, you will only have to purchase a one—way ticket from Texas to Las Vegas.

My other imagined father went to work every day and bought food for his family. He was highly respected by everyone who knew him. He was the pillar of his community, wherever that was. My second real father did not drink, smoke, or curse at his current family (if he had one).

This real father loved my mother before she met her current bastard husband, but I was sure she had just never gotten around to telling her previous lover about me. This fantasy father would put his arm proudly around my shoulders, mess up my hair, and tell me jokes. We laughed a lot together in my fantasies.

My mom was barely pregnant by someone other than Harry when she married, I was convinced, and that was a big family secret. One day, I promised myself, I would search the world and find this perfect father. He would love me just the way I was. In the meantime, I wrote him this letter:

My Dear Mr. (Maybe) Father:

I know this letter will come as a shock to you, but I think I am your son. My mom was barely pregnant when she married her one and only husband, and she probably never told you about me. If you would like to meet me, please send me a letter and we will meet in secret if you prefer. If this letter will harm you and a current family, please just tear it up. I believe that if our meeting is meant to be, no one can stop it, and if it's not meant to be, there is nothing either of us can do to make it happen.

Hoping and praying I'm your son,
James, Tumbleweed, Texas

One of my deepest, darkest secrets (and the source of immense anxiety, pain, and fear of exposure) was that I sucked my thumb until age thirteen. It was after I started school that it immediately became a deep, dark secret. On one occasion while writing in my journal in the closet, I looked up and saw a coat Aunt Taylor had saved and given to Mom when she learned she had no warm winter coat.

That coat was a rich caramel color made of the softest material I had ever felt. The lining was a shiny, slick fabric I would stroke as I sucked my thumb. The comfort the lining of that coat gave me is indescribable.

It smelled like homemade soap—exactly like my mom. I pulled it off the hanger and draped it around my shoulders. For those fleeting, too-short moments, my mother was holding me and cradling me again. She was not concerned about what painful blow would next appear out of the blue, she had no cares in the world, and she had no one to love and protect but me. I did not even feel the oppressive Texas heat in a house with no air conditioning while wearing it.

My secret thumb sucking while stroking and smelling the soft fabric, and the comfort those sensations provided me, became such an addiction that my short trips to the coat in the closet were not enough. I needed a piece of the fabric to rub my nose as I sucked my thumb to comfort me when I went to bed after making sure everything was all right with my mom and brothers.

One day while my mom was hanging clothes on the fence and Harry was gone fishing with his buddies, I took a pair of scissors from an old cigar box that held Mom's thread, went to the closet, and cut out a piece of the lining of the coat in what I thought was an inconspicuous place. Since coats were out of season, it was a while before I got caught.

Quite a while later my "suck rag," as everyone mockingly called it until it completely disintegrated, had fallen on the floor during the night. Mom found it and immediately ran to her closet to locate the missing hole. She dissolved into tears, crying facedown on her bed for what seemed like hours.

Mom finally got up, washed her face, and warned us all not to ever tell Dad I had cut the rag from the lining of her beautiful coat she had carefully kept hidden from him—for two reasons. First, she never wanted Dad to beat me, and second, she was afraid he would accuse her of getting the coat from an imagined boyfriend.

Through the years Harry's biggest hold over me was to threaten to expose my deepest, darkest secret to everyone that I sucked my thumb. I would do almost anything he demanded to keep from experiencing the horror of that emotional disrobing. The evil hold Harry had over me almost daily confirmed the fact that I would have to kill him to stop this evil madness that was beginning to control each waking moment.

Only while in my closet could I admit to myself during the second grade that there was something bad wrong with me. Let me correct that—*everything* was bad wrong with me, and there was no doubt I was fatally flawed.

I did not know what it was, but one key secret and shameful

41

thing I did know was that I did not feel the same way about girls that my peers did. My peers bragged about hating girls. I would have given anything in those early years to have known someone—anyone—I could have asked who could have explained that abnormality to me.

All the girls were my friends. They would confide in me which boys they thought were cute—a subject on which we almost always agreed! One of my best friends, Betsy, the one who gave me the Care Bear, became my protector, constant companion in public, and confidante.

Betsy was always (and still is) much taller, more physically fit, more outgoing, and more courageous than I could ever hope to be. Betsy was not afraid of anyone or anything. She devoted her life to scaring off any older bully who would call me vile names long before she or I knew the meaning of those words.

At that time she would automatically spring into action, not because she always knew the meaning of what they were saying but because of the hateful way they were saying it. Betsy promised to be my protector for life.

Many times Betsy would pull a bully off of me who was pummeling me into the ground for just being me. She and I nicknamed the bullies the Jock Pack, because most of them played sports and acted like a pack of dogs, each following the leader who would start tormenting me.

She gave me too many gifts to count, including my life, on more than one occasion. None of those gifts compares to the gift of three of the most beautiful nieces in the world. Many years later, she fell in love and married my brother Adam.

As strange as it may seem, during those early, often-violent altercations, I vividly remember when a bully would be on top of me, cursing and hitting me repeatedly, that I would become distracted by his great-smelling cologne, hair, crisp, clean-smelling clothes, and new tennis shoes, forgetting the pain and the shame being poured almost daily on my head by Harry like indelible ink from an upside down topless inkwell, permanently staining me for life for all the world to see.

That is about the time that I came to the realization that I was going to be too small, too skinny, too tired, and too sleepy to play sports. I conveniently developed a healthy disdain for all sports and the people who were obsessed with them (often the same boys who were ganging up on me on the playground or on the way home after school).

Even if I had been large enough, for several reasons I could never have played sports anyway. First, because of the lack of nutrition at home, my strength and endurance were limited, especially early in elementary school.

Second, when going too many hours without food, my hands developed a tremor that made me look nervous and scared, even when I was not. I learned at an early age that any indication I was scared meant more frequent beatings and harassment from my predators both young and old.

In addition, and maybe most important of all, sports uniforms were too tight and revealing. My embarrassingly protruding ribs and skinny legs had to remain safely hidden underneath my too-large shirts and baggy pants at all times, whatever the cost.

One of my indelible memories of those years was of being ravenously hungry most of the time. I also vividly remember, oddly enough, not usually being especially bothered by the pain that went with the hunger. Feeling the pain meant I was still alive. Feeling it was confirmation that I had not yet starved to death, and Harry had not killed me during a drunken rage.

When I was in the second grade, I stole a spiral notebook from Aunt Rosie's desk to document a seizure I had witnessed Harry bring on my mom. I started writing in that notebook, but it was too large to fit behind the sheetrock in my closet. Because of the deep, dark secrets I was writing each night, I knew I had to hide it somewhere else.

The neighbors down the street had been evicted from their

home by the sheriff. They left after an altercation, and all their belongings were hauled to the end of the driveway as garbage. A stained, ragged box spring mattress was part of the valuable treasure that I spotted on my way home from school.

We waited until after dark and Harry, my brothers, and I dragged the mattress to our house. It was badly stained with urine and mold, but Mom and I drenched it in vinegar and bleach water and put it in the backyard in the sun to dry. Since I had been sleeping on the floor, it was like Christmas Day to me. I wrote a letter that night to my mom's god that she loved so much, thanking him for the blessing, and stuffed it securely in my new hiding place.

The kitchen floors in our house, probably built in the 1930s, had badly stained white/brownish or yellowed and faded asbestos linoleum that was curling up, and on which I regularly tripped, cutting and/or bruising myself. The bedroom floors were unfinished wooden planks that had dried and warped. This flooring quickly became the convenient excuse I gave for all bruises on my body to those who noticed them, anywhere, anytime.

There were holes in the cracked linoleum floors and cracks between the wooden planks in the wooden floors where I stuffed rags to keep out rats and insects and to keep in the little heat we would have on occasion when my mom's disability check would arrive and the past-due bill could be paid. We had no air conditioning in the house, so we sweltered eight months of most years.

Weeds would quickly grow around the rags. Part of every Saturday house cleaning was to pull the easy weeds and cut the tough ones with a pair of scissors and re-stuff the rags. The lining on my box spring mattress had a tear in it where I kept my clothes to make it softer to sleep on and to cushion the coils from protruding through the cover and hurting or cutting my bony body.

I wrapped my notebook in my carefully folded clothes and returned it to the inside of the mattress after each entry. There are many entries in my journal over several years that are almost identical to each other. The entries would read, "Dad bloodied Mom's face today. Dad called Mom a whore today. Dad begged Mom for forgiveness today, saying, 'I'm so sorry. You know how much I love you and the boys. That was not the real me that did that. I will make it up to y'all, I promise.'"

That promise, borne of guilt, would last until payday, or until one of Dad's buddies dropped by with a six- or twelve-pack of beer, and the cycle would start all over again.

My mom excused Harry each time, telling him and us it was all her fault. How I longed for my mom to put a stop to the charade we were all living, but back in those years I saw her as a trembling, captured, defenseless bird, taunted in the cage that imprisoned her.

From the second grade through the fourth grade, I wrote almost every afternoon in my closet, sometimes only a line or two, sharing my secret thoughts, pain, and the deepest longings of my soul in that notebook.

My pink Care Bear with the rainbow on its belly was always close by.

CHAPTER 5

CHEATED CHRISTMAS

Before Christmas in 1989, my mom had pulled us aside, explaining that although we didn't have any money for toys, it was important that we remember the birth of the baby Jesus. When I asked about Santa Claus, Harry chuckled loudly, mocking Santa's deep laugh of ho, ho, ho, and then said, "You are stupider than I thought you were. There is no Santa Claus. It's just best you learn that right now."

That was not the first time I thought at my young age that he had lied to me. I refused to take those hurtful words in, not wanting to give up my one last hope for toys.

We had been invited to a church dinner with all the trimmings on the Saturday before Christmas on Monday. We really looked forward to it. The food was so good, cooked by all the ladies in the church, and we could have as much as we wanted. I don't remember being that full and satisfied since.

I tasted my first piece of homemade coconut crème pie, and it was the best thing I had ever tasted. I was feeling great until I ate a second piece forced on me by a kind lady who wanted to wash the pie tin and insisted I eat it. The result was my first excruciatingly painful lesson in the importance of moderation.

On the next afternoon, Christmas Eve 1989, several local

firemen knocked on our door. They brought fruit, bags of nuts, and toys. We kids were elated!

Harry was drunk, and he instantly became abusive. He asked them if they were insinuating that he could not take care of his family. He shoved a bag of oranges back at one of the firemen but luckily did not injure him. He screamed and cursed for them to get out of his house and take all the gifts to truly needy kids. We kids knew not to cry nor say a word.

On Christmas day around noon when he got up, Harry announced he was going to get some money he had loaned to a friend, saying in one of his rare kind moments, "I might have enough to bring y'all back some toys."

He left, and we didn't see him until the next Saturday morning. Where he was or what he had been doing is anyone's guess. My mom never asked him to explain what had happened or where he had been. We kids never asked what happened to the toys because we knew even at our young ages that his promises were just lies in the first place.

Mom's best friend since childhood was named Anna. She visited occasionally, usually between failed relationships that always made her down on her luck. That same year she came and helped Mom cook pinto beans and cornbread for our Christmas dinner and came and went off and on until New Year's morning. She was a party-hearty-type woman who, unlike my mom, drank, smoked pot, and flirted with Harry right in front of my mom and us kids. She had the reputation of someone who'd been with any man in the county who was drunk enough to be with her.

She was not attractive at all. She had teeth rotting at the root and a large, bulbous nose. She was skinny and had small boobs. When she and Harry would smoke pot, drink beer, and dance seductively to country western music in front of all of us, they started looking at each other in a way that alarmed me. I walked out on the porch where they were smoking pot, and she was telling

Harry in horrifying detail all about her sexual skills that drove the men crazy.

I looked straight at Harry's groin just below my eye level, and there was a noticeable bulge under the front of his pants with a wet circle around it. I ran inside to the bathroom and threw up my dinner.

Later that night Anna and Harry, loopy from smoking pot, popping pills, drinking beer, and increasingly filthy talk, got so drunk that Mom made a pallet for my brothers and me and insisted that Anna go get in my brothers' bed down the hall. Mom kept begging Harry to come to bed with her, probably because she saw him staring down the hall with that same weird expression that had alarmed me earlier. He mumbled, acting like he was falling asleep in his chair, and Mom stormed off to bed by herself.

A few hours later I heard weird noises from the bedroom where Anna was supposed to be sleeping. I listened at the door for a minute until I heard Harry moaning and groaning, saying terrible things and comparing my mom's anatomy unfavorably to Anna's in the most explicit detail as he had sex with my mom's best friend. My hatred for him was indescribable in that moment.

I went to Mom's room and told her I was hearing weird noises. Mom rushed down the hall, flung open the door to the bedroom that had no lock, and flipped on the light, and Anna and Harry were having sex, with Mom and all of us kids right there in the house.

My mom flew into the biggest rage I have ever seen anyone throw in my life. She was pulling Anna's hair, scratching her eyes, punching her in the face, and kicking her with all her might. Anna kept screaming, "Stop, Jane! It isn't what it looks like! Let me explain!" I looked out the window, and by that time Harry was streaking barefoot and naked down the street under the full moon. Why, I asked myself, wasn't Mom saying or doing anything to Harry?

We heard that Anna left for Colorado the next day. And as far as anyone knows, she never came back. I never told Mom what I overheard Harry say. Maybe I should have, or maybe I was afraid it would just hurt her too deeply. I could also see her blaming herself and forgiving him one more time anyway.

The day after Christmas, Uncle Jim came to the house with their old black-and- white TV. Uncle Jim had bought Aunt Rosie a new color one for Christmas so she could watch *As the World Turns* in color. I never knew Aunt Rosie to turn that TV off from then on. She sat right in front of that television, day and a lot of nights when she would fall asleep on the couch in front of it, all during my childhood.

I watched my first Oprah program on that TV during the holidays and fell in love with her outside and her inside. She was so beautiful, compassionate, and understanding. The stories of her childhood traumas touched my heart. Although our experiences were somewhat different in the details, we both had experienced and knew profoundly the pain of suffering.

That following spring, 1990, I wrote my first hand-printed letter to Oprah, right after an all-too-typical incident. When in a drunken rage, one of Harry's favorite things was to hit the kitchen table so hard it would crack or break a leg or be destroyed completely. When he sobered up, he would deny ever having done it, usually casting the blame on me while proceeding with a slipshod repair, complaining in disgust all the while.

Since the Big God was so remote, unseen, unavailable, and evidently too busy for me while looking after and saving the entire world, I found an earthly replacement on television. My God was a black female. She was someone who was always surprising her fans with makeovers and putting smiles on the faces of depressed, unattractive, lonely, or poor fans.

My God became Oprah, and unlike the Big God, she had an address where I could write to her, and she could write me back. My first request to Oprah was for a new, sturdy kitchen table.

Dear Oprah:

How are you? I am fine. My first name is James. One day I will change my middle name 'cause I was named for a neighbor guy who is mean and hurts me. I don't like to hear the word. My first name came from my uncle, and he is nice to me. So it's okay to call me James. I have a lot of other names too, but they are mostly bad so I won't tell you what they are. Not yet anyway. Maybe one day. My uncle Jim gave Aunt Rosie a new colored TV for Christmas. She said she just had to watch <u>As the World Turns</u> in color so she gave us her old one for Christmas, and boy were we happy when Uncle Jim gave us her old black and white one cause my dad lost his job and we don't get no toys or a tree. My dad usually don't like Aunt Rosie, but now he likes her better cause he can watch wrestling on TV and drink beer. I hate wrestling as much as my dad hates you and your show, but when he's watching wrestling and screaming and cussing at the TV, he ain't screaming or cussing at me and my mom and brothers, and that's a good thing. I saw your show the other day and I like it, and I wanted to write to tell you. Also, if you need a mom to help out for another show, please put my mama on your list. She needs a new table. Our table got broke the other day when my mom slipped and fell into it after she mopped. I told my mom I was going write to you and she just hollered from the kitchen for me to be sure to tell you I am your fan and she likes you too. I like that word fan. That's one of the first things I'll buy my mama when I get a job. It's just what you are like to me, a cool breeze in the hot summer. My dad is gone fishing with his buddies or she couldn't holler nothin' to me.

Sincerely,
James, your friend and fan in Tumbleweed, Texas

In my second, almost instantaneous request after a sleepless night of reviewing in my mind what that first mailed letter had said, I panicked and wrote another letter.

Dear Oprah,

I wish I could tell you I am fine, but I ain't. I'm so scared I can't sleep. I'm sorry I mailed my letter to you. I forgot to tell you never tell my mom and dad I ask you for a table and never tell my dad I am writing you. Please, please, answer my prayer. If you decide to send us a new table, please send it without your name on the box. That way my dad would think the postman left it at the wrong house and he would laugh and not get mad at me for asking for a handout. Beggars get handouts, and we may be poor but we ain't no beggars.

Sincerely,
James, your friend and fan in Tumbleweed, Texas

Looking back, maybe a new table would be a tangible representation of a new beginning of mended relationships and/ or a firm foundation to hold and protect the already insufficient food that barely sustained our physical lives.

Maybe around a new table we could have safe, happy meals and the bonding and memories I heard others brag about. Sitting around a new table, I could see us laughing, talking, and loving one another during our meals. That new, sturdy kitchen table represented a new beginning to me in so many ways.

What I didn't send to Oprah was a poem I wrote after one of Harry's table-smashing incidents:

Maybe he'll die in his sleep one night,
Poisoned by a rattlesnake bite.
After we bury him we'll be able
To buy a brand new kitchen table.

In that first request to Oprah, I had lied about how the table had gotten broken. Never had I, nor would I, let any outside person know ours was not the perfect family. When I soon learned the Ten Commandments in Sunday school and heard a sermon on the importance of truthfulness, I knew in that moment why my request had not been granted.

I promised myself I would start telling the truth but just not *all* the truth. Some facts could always be left out without telling an outright lie. I scolded and berated myself for needlessly having fabricated a false story about how it had gotten broken in the first place. I had been my own worst enemy.

What I soon accepted (as letter after letter received no answer) was that Oprah was similar to the Big God. She was also very busy and could not help every poor person who asked her for a favor. I started drawing pictures for her and decorating my letters with colorful stick cartoon characters.

I never gave up hope she would answer my letters, as I visualized her walking to her mailbox in a white fluffy robe and house shoes her hair in curlers, filling both her arms with all the letters she would get each day and mine falling on the ground in its splendid decorated glory. She would then lean over, pick it up, read it, and send us that new table.

Although I never heard from Oprah through the years, I learned so much from this experience. In fact, I credit it for saving my life on more than one occasion by giving me the strength to live one more day. I learned that we don't always get what we ask for. I learned that people can, and often will, disappoint us when they don't even know they are doing so. I learned that when we replace the Big God with a human one, we set ourselves up for disappointment.

I learned that just the slightest glimmer of hope could help ameliorate the hopelessness and helplessness all children experience sometime during their childhood. There was always another letter to be written, another day to check the mailbox, and disappointment to be shared in stolen moments with my journal. Mr. Boles, my Sunday school teacher, had told us if we wanted God to forgive us we had to forgive our brothers.

During that lesson I remember wondering if God were confused about genders. I remember thinking that another word meaning both brothers and sisters would make me feel so much better. Neither the word *friend* nor the word *enemy* fit in every situation. I was grown before I heard the word *sibling*. Anyway, even though Oprah was not a brother, I decided I better forgive her. So I did. I love her to this day.

Dear Oprah,

It's me again, James, your friend in Tumbleweed, Texas. I hope I'm not bothering you 'cause I never want you to be mad at me. My aunt Rosie found your address for me. I told her I wrote you and told you I like your show, but she laughed and said Oprah ain't gonna answer no letter from a kid. Maybe she's right. God never answers my prayers but praying is talking, and there is no place I can write to God. Anyways, I like writing better than talking 'cause I never get hit or screamed at when writing, except sometimes after when somebody snoops and reads it. I try to write like a man so maybe that's why. My teacher liked my story about my summer vacation. She said I might be a writer one day. I was so mad at myself 'cause I just started crying. The tears just dropped from my eyes for no reason.

Ever morning I feel okay till I get to school, and then I feel sick. I go to the nurse and she gets mad cause I ain't got no fever. She says I'm faking and I look just fine to her. She also got mad and told me I'm faking 'cause I have a spelling test I have not studied for. She is so dumb. Spelling tests are on Fridays anyways, and today is Wednesday. I can already spell all the words for this week anyways.

You are the only one I can tell why I get sick, and I know you will never tell nobody nothing I ever tell you.

Well here it goes. I think I'm a girl, so why was I born a boy? I'm smaller than my brothers and all the girls in my class, and all the boys at school call me bad names and spit on me. Also I cry about everything. That is one thing I don't like about being a girl if I am one. Eddie says he's going to fix me good ever day when school is out 'cause I'm a faggot. I don't know what that means. All I know is that it's bad and I don't have no one but you I can ask. My friend Betsy walked home with me today, and nobody bothers me when she's with me. I never want to go anywhere without her for the rest of my life.

Before my uncle Henry started drinking today, he got real mad and told me to stop throwing a ball and walking like a girl, but I don't know what that means. I can't ask him before he starts drinking or he'll get mad, but after he has drank four beers he acts like a girl too. Could I walk like a man if I had four beers? Could Uncle Henry be my real daddy?

I wish I had God's address so I could write to him and ask him to ask you to write me back. Prayer does not work and is not a good idea. I run home every day after school to get the mail before my dad finds it. I won't never be able to write you again if he finds a letter from you first. I ain't got no reason to think there is a God anyways besides you.

Besides Nancy, Carlotta, and Betsy, you are my best friend.

Sincerely,
James, your friend in Tumbleweed, Texas

PS: I'm sending you a stamp from Aunt Rosie's desk. I ain't telling her I took it, but I promised myself to pay her back when I get a job.

CHAPTER 6

TOY SOLDIER

The main memory of my first year in the third grade cuts me to the core. After some experience at the Love Center, I avoided unique clothes that could be identified as a younger siblings' of a friend that had been donated. Once one of the rich kids, whose father owned a large company just outside of town, screamed to everyone that I was wearing a shirt his little sister had outgrown and his mom had donated to the Love Center.

I ran to the nurse at school, crying and upset. Between my uncontrollable sobs, she scolded me for faking too many illnesses and sent me right back to class, where everyone continued laughing and taunting me. As much as I loved that shirt, I angrily shoved it, crying audibly like an abandoned child, into a garbage can on the way home.

In September of 1991, the decision was made to have me repeat the third grade. Mrs. Henderson, my teacher, reportedly told my parents it would be a good thing because I was so small for my age, and the teachers had fear about my personal safety, both in and after school.

I never knew if these were truly the real reasons, but the boys who had been promoted to the fourth grade were convinced that it was because I was not just a fag but I was also dumb. Sadly, I believed them since the facts were clearly on their side.

I loved my next (second) third-grade teacher, Ms. Patterson. She had the most beautiful long, shiny black hair I had ever seen. I loved getting close enough to her to smell her perfume.

She smelled just like the broken-down fence on my walk home from school when it was covered with honeysuckles. I wanted to be her. She used a lot of words I had never heard before, and I often had to ask Betsy to find out from her brother what a word meant she had just used.

I went to school with a lot of bruises that year, and my teacher would always sincerely ask what had happened to me. I'm sure she was amazed at how many excuses I could come up with to take the focus away from my home life.

My spelling improved a lot from the beginning of the year to the end of the year, as reflected in my journal. Ms. Patterson would instantly make up poems to help us learn the difference in similar-sounding words. Everyone knew about my Care Bear. And the only poem I remember, created just for me after misspelling bear on a spelling test, was, "A bear cannot be bare, unless you shave off his hair."

Ms. Patterson called us all "Precious," and that was the first time I had ever heard that word. By the mere tone of her voice, I knew what it meant without even asking Betsy. I loved it when she called on me. I never even minded her correcting me. In retrospect, I'm sure I'd do something wrong just so I could hear her say, "Now, Precious, go back to your seat." When I hear that word today, her face immediately comes to mind, and I get a warm feeling.

During college Ms. Patterson had backpacked with schoolmates through Europe for a semester and a summer. Her descriptions of Rome, Paris, Vienna, and Dublin mesmerized me. I promised myself that one day I would be able to visit those exotic places. Schoolwork, thankfully, was easy that year because I had already learned what was being taught and fun also because of that special teacher, my second year in the third grade.

One day when I finally visit those exotic spots in person, I'm sure I'll have a feeling of déjà vu, since in my vivid imagination I have already toured those faraway places myself with a backpack on my back, staying in hostels.

During that year I vividly remember hating the weekends and holidays when there was no school, because at school there was food and distractions from my problems at home. Summers were the hardest.

In the summer of 1993 before I started the fifth grade that fall, I became careless with my journal. One day I had been playing in my heavy black sweats with my brothers in hundred-plus degree temperature and ran into the house to change into my silky black soccer shorts with unraveling seams, the ones my mom called, "Your air conditioned shorts," that had finally gotten dry on the fence.

As I entered the house, Harry was napping on his alcohol-drenched couch, open Natural Light can on the floor, wet with beer dripping from its lip. He had obviously passed out, his fingers letting go of a partially finished can.

I tiptoed quietly to my room. I stepped out of my sweat-soaked, hot black sweat pants. I put my right leg in my shorts. The next thing I knew, I remember waking up face down on the floor, lying in a pool of blood, with my mom screaming, "Stop! You're going to kill him!" Harry lunged at her, cursing, while ordering her out of the room. As always, she meekly complied.

He started slapping me and grabbing at me. I knew not to allow a tear to come out no matter how bad one wanted to. Thankfully my tears were secure behind the dam of secrets and shame that life had built, brick by brick, inside of me. A break in that dam would have just encouraged additional blows, more name-calling, and even possible death.

Harry grabbed me and threw me around screaming, "What the hell are you thinking writing down these muthafucking lies? This shit can really get me and your mother in a lot of trouble!

Is this what you want, you faggot bitch? You like hurting people, huh, you goddamned fucking fag?

"How does this feel," he screamed as he slammed me into the closet door, slapping my chest and face with one hand while he held me against the wall by my neck with the other hand. He continued to shout angrily, "This is just a tiny taste of the pain you are trying to cause your mother. Don't ever let me hear you say you love her again, you fucking two-faced little sissy bastard!"

The pain finally became too much as the air was leaving my body, boring a hole in the dyke of hatred that held back my tears. The tears gushed as I began to cry. Instead of physically killing me, as I had so greatly feared, he yelled, "You will never amount to anything, much less a real man! You will always be a goddamned, muthaloving, muthafucking crybaby fag!"

He let go of my neck, bent down to the floor, picked up the now dog-eared notebook, and held it up to the light, and with an orange Bic lighter, he lit the corners on fire. He reached behind him on my bed, and the blood drained from my body as I watched him light my beloved Care Bear on fire.

As I watched my memories, thoughts, and dreams, my beloved bear and poems burn in such a few seconds, I could not help but try and fight to rescue my journal and bear. I failed, losing all I held dear in the wink of an eye.

Mom warned me later that night, whispering secretly away from Dad, "When he does stuff like that, just stay quiet and still, and never, ever—no matter how bad you want to—fight back."

For the next few months, I began to recreate the thoughts and entries from my burned journal in a new journal I bought at TG&Y, a local variety store, with change I took from my mom's purse. I turned to a page in the middle of the journal and continued the list of the whys and how I should kill him. From that day forward, I always put my journal back in its hiding place after making those entries.

I look back and think I was on the brink of a nervous breakdown when a kind older couple surnamed Lay came to stay with their grandkids next door to us while their daughter and son-in-law went on business and leisure trips without the kids. Mrs. Lay's first name was Dee (GranDee to the grandchildren). GranDee disliked her married name, Dee Lay. She was not a procrastinator and despised anyone who was, so that's why she'd always insert her maiden name, Holcomb, when saying her name.

GranDee was just an overgrown kid herself and would make us kids laugh so hard we would cry. Years later, every time I saw Phyllis Diller on television, I would say, "She looks and acts just like GranDee!"

PapaDee was more introverted and was a man of few words, but he had a very kind heart. On his first visit he made all of us kids a whistle he had whittled out of wood while sitting on his back porch. He etched our initials in each one so we would know which one was ours. I urged him to leave out my middle initial. The whistle was the first gift I can remember that I didn't have to share, and no one could argue was this. I hid my new treasure in the hiding place behind the sheetrock in my closet, along with my journal. It later became an important item on my list of reasons I should kill Harry.

GranDee adopted my brothers and me over the back fence each stay and insisted my brothers and I call her GranDee as well. She would invite us to go to her kitchen for chocolate chip cookies hot out of the oven washed down with ice-cold milk.

We were threatened by Harry never to go inside a neighbor's house because they could be perverts luring us to terrible fates. GranDee understood and handed us freshly baked chocolate chip cookies over the back fence. They would be so hot they would almost burn our tongue. As we bit into them, the melted chips would drip in warm strings down on the front of our clothes and shoes.

I always wondered how Mom always knew why we were uncharacteristically not all that hungry at suppertime. Maybe moms really do have invisible eyes in the backs of their heads, I remember thinking to myself.

One of the fondest memories of the Lays' occasional visits was the time they brought their grandchildren a new tiny reddish-brown and white Chihuahua as a gift. The puppy's mom had died at the litter's birth.

Resting in GranDee's palm, that tiny puppy looked like a ball of peanut brittle.

GranDee offered a prize of a bag of marbles to the one of us coming up with the best name for the puppy. Their grandchildren were two and three years old and too young to participate in the contest. I thought on it all night and wrote in my journal:

I love GranDee and I love her grandkids' new puppy. The puppy should be named LayDee after her. I hate my name, too. I hope this makes GranDee feel better about her name.

Adam wanted to name her Killer, and Joseph thought the name Gorilla would scare off all the big dogs. We all had a big laugh over those names. When I unfolded the piece of school paper I had folded up into a tiny square with my entry into the contest printed out in large letters, I handed it to GranDee.

She gasped in delight, reached down, picked me up, and swirled me around, laughing and crying at the same. She never said it, but I knew I was the hands-down winner of the contest. With a secret wink toward me, GranDee gave a bag of marbles to each of us for our efforts, and baby LayDee had a new name.

The Lays had bought a baby bottle and powdered formula at the feed store for LayDee. She became my baby. I mixed her bottle and fed that puppy each bottle until she thought I was her mama. Adam and Joseph would take their turn but would quickly hand puppy and bottle to me, probably partially afraid of the fragility of the puppy and partially embarrassed at the uncomfortably way-too-sissy role they were being forced into playing.

The Lays never missed church, and one Wednesday night

they were gone for three hours attending services and socializing afterward. I was traumatized and in denial when I saw that Harry was out in the backyard burying something small in a paper sack in the hole he had just made us dig. I was frozen in fear.

We all searched for that dog unsuccessfully for days before I could accept the truth. I later became sure the dog had probably awakened Harry from sleeping off a bender. To say we kids loved that dog would be an understatement. I still cry when I think of the cruel fate that adored pet met.

If Harry would do that to LayDee, I was further convinced that he would also do it to my mom, my brothers, and even me. That's the only dog I remember or suspected that he buried, because his favorite victims were cats. When a cat came on our property, it was a foregone conclusion that us boys would be ordered to dig another deep hole. A few weeks earlier I had entered this poem in my journal when I caught Harry in the act:

> Harry knocked a kitten in the head
> For crying and whining to be fed.
> You better take heed
> For your next bad deed,
> I promise I'll kill you instead.

I swore to myself during that time to never, ever, be unkind to a pet. I hated Harry more than usual that night and added another reason to my growing list of why he had to be killed.

My obsession with killing my dad was always lessened during the times a teacher would have us write a story. One such assignment came at the perfect time. I desperately needed a respite from my growing list of reasons to kill Harry. I knew how much Oprah loved reading and books, so I always sent her reports of the stories I had written.

Dear Oprah:

I know I will hear from you soon—I just have that good feeling. I can see you on TV so I know you are fine and looking so pretty every day. You can't see me so I want you to know I'm fine too. I hope you have a stamp so you can answer me and tell me you like my story. I like writing better than talking. Once you've said something, it's almost impossible to take it back. When I'm writing about the bad things, I can make it turn out happy. I get the same feeling I have when my brothers let me be king of the world after I beat 'em up. I see on TV how you love stories and cry when they are sad, so here goes one. My teacher told us to write a story today. She said to pretend we was a toy in a department store window. What toy would we be? Who would buy us, and what would happen next? She said to make the story either happy or sad, but it had to have a happy ending. I know I'm really a girl because I could not stop crying while I was writing my story until the happy ending when I could smile again. Nobody but a girl would cry at something made up.

I decided I was a toy soldier in a department store window and these two kids come along and bought me, and they took me home and called me bad names. One cut my hair all off with a pair of scissors they stole from their mama's sewing box, and one stabbed me with a pencil over and over, pulling as they stabbed to tear me, opening up my chest, then they threw me down the stairs and my eyeball falls out.

Them kids fell all over each other running down the stairs and I wanted so bad for that to be the sad part of my story, but that part was not about the toy soldier. I will write another really good story about them falling down the stairs. It might be my very first story I ever write without a happy ending. Anyways, them two took turns jumping up and down on me until my insides was coming out, and they laughed so hard it woke their mama up from a nap.

Their mama, Mrs. B. Q. Smith, was so mad she gave them the beating of their lives. While they was squalling to high heaven, she picked me up and looked in my face all mean and mad, shook me with all her might, and then she screamed, "You ain't any good to nobody now no way." Then she threw me as hard as she could into a fiery furnace like Mr. Boles told us about in Sunday school. Mrs. B. Q. Smith jumped back, almost falling down 'cause when I hit the fire it spit and popped, and then them flames got hotter and hotter.

But I was made of asbestos pants, and I did not burn.

You can buy me from a toy store.
You can think I'm yours to change.

You can stab me to the core.
You can make me look all strange.

You can throw me down the stairs.
You can make my eye fall out.

You can cut off all my hairs.
You can curse me as you shout.

You can stomp me
with your shoes.
Till my body falls apart.

You can stab with
force and bruise.
In both ways you can
break my heart.

You can fling me in the fire
Without worry or concern.

But I'm made of asbestos pants,
And I will not burn.

Dear Oprah:

I decided maybe my letters are too long so I am sending a short one today. We've been learning about parts of speech, and I only have three quick questions because I know you will know the answers and there's no one else I can ask and I will do anything you tell me to do.

1. Is faggot a verb or a noun?
2. Is it something I say or do?
   If you think it's something I am
3. Is there anything I can do?

I go to my mailbox every day.
God let there be a letter, I pray.
I fight back a tear,
Then say, "Oprah, dear,
For your time and your stamp I will pay."

Sincerely,
James, your friend and fan in Tumbleweed, Texas

No one could have guessed how badly I wanted to run away from home. But in reality, running away was impossible. If I committed a selfish act like that, who would protect my mom and brothers from this monster who called himself our dad? Who would distract him when he was beating on my mom or brothers so he would quit hurting them and pivot to me?

About that time, Harry disappeared for several days before Mom's check arrived. My brothers and I were always hungry, especially on the weekends. Now that we were abandoned orphans for no telling how long, I had to find a way to feed us.

CHAPTER 7

PLAYING DENTIST

After going to Vacation Bible School and attending Sunday school for a few weeks, I began having numerous questions about religion, God, Jesus, miracles, and my eternal destiny just for starters. I was at the same time beginning to be fascinated with the subject of love. I had a serious crush on a classmate named Todd. He was one of the smartest people I had ever met. He smelled like the Old Spice he would sneak from his father's medicine chest before coming to church. He was a lot taller than I was, and he also hated sports.

This was the very first time any boy had showed me kindness by touching my hand tenderly in church and letting me know he thought I was cute. Girls had been chasing me down since the first grade and kissing me, and I hated it. Still theologically worried about who I was, why God made me the way I was, and especially where I was going to spend eternity, I wrote two poems in church one Sunday morning after Sunday school instead of listening to the pastor's sermon. I promised myself I would share this first one only with my journal:

If God is love
And I love Todd,
Between the two of us is God.

I then had a flash of eleven-year-old genius and reconsidered my promise. I would put the first poem on notebook paper, put it in my pocket, and take it with me to Sunday school the next Sunday morning and show it to Mr. Boles. He would then know my secret sexual confusion and would be able to counsel me. I would never have been able to come up with the words even if I had had the correct vocabulary—or the courage—to tell him that I was really worried about my developing sexual identity.

Once again I started a letter to Oprah to tell her about my inner turmoil, but lacking courage to ask her what I was most worried about, the letter turned into something else less threatening that I was also worried about. The scarier questions could always wait for another letter.

Dear Oprah,

I'm so scared I could cry for two reasons. First, my dad will beat me if I don't go to church so he can have some peace and quiet, and if I go I will tell you why I am scared. Mr. Boles told us to learn the Ten Commandments and we will say them all together before the church next Sunday. I only miss one or two now when I'm not looking at the answers, so that's not my problem.

I'm not too scared just about standing in front of the church neither. What I'm scared about is my clothes and shoes and I'm afraid they will laugh at me.

On your show you had a fashion expert who said any girl can look good and she showed how a scarf or a hat or a belt could dress up and cover up even the cheapest clothes. She was talking about girls, not boys. If I was a girl I would know what to do just because of your show.

Is there anything a boy can do to look better so no one will laugh?

Here are the Moses Ten Commandments in case you forgot:

1. Thou shalt put God first.
2. Thou shalt worship only God.
3. Thou shalt use God's name with respect.
4. Thou shalt remember God's Sabbath.
5. Thou shalt respect your parents.
6. Thou shalt not kill.
7. Thou shalt be faithful in marriage.
8. Thou shalt not steal.
9. Thou shalt not lie.
10. Thou shalt not envy others.

Sincerely,
James, your friend in Tumbleweed, Texas

PS: What is your favorite commandment? It will be mine too unless it's thou shalt not kill.

In my journal that night I wrote:

> The gift I want more than any other
> Is a father who respects my mother.

I wrote another letter the next day.

Dear Oprah,

I just seen another show about how to be a good parent. I made my own Ten Commandments list as well. These are a few of the things your experts never said. Maybe they just forgot.

Ten Commandments for Dads
1. Do not spit on your kids.
2. Do not slap them in their face.
3. Do not pick them up by one arm.
4. Do not hurt their mama.
5. Do not hit them in the head.
6. Do not cuss at them.
7. Do not call them stupid.
8. Do not pinch them really, really hard at their grandpa's funeral.
9. Do not get drunk and call them a sissy or a faggot.
10. Do not tell them to stop walking like a girl (unless they are a girl).

Sincerely,
James, your fan and friend in Tumbleweed, Texas

After church that day Betsy ran up to me and showed me a potholder maker she had just received for her birthday. She showed me the beautiful colored loops she would thread on a metal form back and forth in a braided square. In just a few minutes, sitting on the back pew, she had a perfectly formed potholder with a loop sticking out of one corner to hang it on a nail in the kitchen.

I lay in bed awake all night planning our new business. The next morning, in my mind, we were soon to be famous—not yet knowing the proper words but fully understanding the basic concepts—wealthy manufacturers and capitalists! My next serious challenge was to share the plan with Betsy the next day at school and sell her on the idea.

At first Betsy was underwhelmed. I was devastated by her

negativity and lack of enthusiasm. *How could she not see the big picture*, I wondered. When I asked her, Betsy explained my idea sounded too much like selling, and she was profoundly against the entire idea of selling things. She said, "Selling is begging people to buy something they probably don't want in the first place, and no one will ever catch me begging or call me a beggar."

I spent two days at lunch and recess explaining to her all the things she used and how someone had made them, someone had sold them, and someone had bought them for her. She finally gave in and said, "Okay, I'll do it if you let me do the making, and you do all the selling."

During that meeting of the minds, she explained once more, just to be sure I understood, that since she was furnishing the loops and making the widgets, she should be in charge of making things, and I would have to be in charge of selling the final product.

We could not wait for the weekend! I told her to make as many as she could in the evenings after school, and we would both start with the neighbors on Saturday morning.

Saturday morning came, and Betsy hid in the bushes at the side of a porch and I, shaking all over, knocked on the first door. We decided to start with strangers, so if we were told no, we wouldn't have to avoid and/or hate a relative for the rest of our lives. We had a long discussion about which relatives that would most likely be. They were, coincidentally, the ones we already hated, and we had absolutely no plans for changing our minds on that subject.

Most of the people were really kind to us. We soon learned that when people didn't have two quarters to buy one of our treasured goods, we would offer to barter. One elderly widowed neighbor lady was so kind admiring our handiwork, but she was having a hard time surviving herself since her husband had recently died.

I was starving that day. She had a beautiful apple tree in her yard, and I offered to trade a potholder for five apples (one for

Mom, one for Adam, one for Joseph, one for Betsy, and one for me) from her tree.

She countered, saying, "Why don't you take five apples that have already fallen from the tree for each of you, and we've got a deal?" She was delighted, and so were we! I didn't know it at the time, but I had just disproved the often-quoted theory, "You will never get more than you ask for!"

We quickly ate two apples each, and I raced home to give my mom and two brothers the remaining apples. My mom interrogated me as if I were a criminal. Stealing apples was a major criminal offense in Mom's book. I would have been punished severely if I had gotten caught committing it. I swore on my life that I had not stolen the apples. Finally after many moments of harsh words and my promises, she took my word and let it go. I'm still trying to find an apple that tasted as good as those did that day.

One day we hit the jackpot. Mrs. Lamb was a sweet Christian lady who was one of the substitute drivers for the bus that picked us up for Sunday school. She almost picked me up off the porch, hugging and squeezing me and blessing my heart when she opened the door. She bought all five potholders we had with us.

As all businesses do, we quickly ran into a dilemma. We were now out of loops after Mrs. Lamb's large order. The TG&Y, our favorite variety store, had a large package for $1.49, but that meant we had to sell three potholders for fifty cents to buy more loops.

We sadly walked to the TG&Y and bought a package of loops, begrudgingly depleting our precious tin can of cash. This was our first painful lesson in, "It takes money to make money," unaware of the fact that we'd make far more from our purchase than we spent. I'm still not good at math.

The next time she picked us up on the bus, Mrs. Lamb asked Betsy and me to stay behind when the other kids got off the bus. She told us she liked her potholders so much that she would like to place an order for Christmas gifts! We had about three months to make twenty-five red and green potholders! We both first panicked at the thought of how much it would cost us to buy the special loops for that many.

I saw the frightened look on Betsy's face and instinctively poked her with my elbow when she almost spilled the beans by turning down her offer. I talked over Betsy's voice, thanked Mrs. Lamb calmly (my outsides definitely not matching my insides) and assured her we were very capable of filling her order. I had absolutely no idea how I would make good on my promise.

Betsy and I had an emergency company board meeting and decided every time she made three potholders, we'd sell one and we'd put two in Mrs. Lamb's box. I negotiated with Mrs. Lamb, after a bus ride, to buy five each time we completed them, and she agreed. Pretty soon, our first large order was completed and paid for. Our tin can started jingling once again with even more cash. We were, without a doubt in our young minds, on the road to great riches.

Predictably, like most start-up companies, we had our first fight over money. While thinking of ways we could increase our business, a teenaged young man came to our door selling cleaning supplies. Harry cursed him out and shouted for him to get off his porch.

I ran out the back door and followed him until we were both out of Harry's sight. I learned that with a twenty-five-dollars investment for samples of cleaning supplies both to sell and use in a new service business, Betsy and I could earn a higher rate of return than with our potholder business, and we didn't have to make anything! This was also a business I could be passionate about since I loved to clean so much.

Betsy had a meltdown. Betsy's tolerance for risk was much lower than mine. Her passion for cleaning was also lacking. In fact, as it turned out, her tolerance for each was sadly zero. We had not yet heard of conflict resolution, mediation, arbitration, or compromise. Betsy won that fight that day and our fledgling cleaning supply business was no more, but many years later I helped work my way through mortuary school by cleaning apartments and houses for friends. Timing really is everything.

After Halloween that year, we started making potholders for all the ladies in our family. By the time we filled Mrs. Lamb's order and made our own, we started running out of loops. Another fight broke out, and we decided our friendship meant more than any business venture. We divided up the spoils, shook hands, and became a statistic in the "most businesses fail in the first year" maxim.

Dear Oprah,

I saw your show on why most new businesses fail, and you are right. In fact Betsy and me we have still never met anyone as smart as you. We was doing real good in our business selling potholders, but we had a big fight over money and I decided I could start my own cleaning business one day and maybe get as rich as you. Most girls I know could not get rich like you 'cause they just mostly want to talk and complain instead of keeping on doing something.

I hope you are real and not trick TV like the moon landing 'cause I know if you made it we can too. Please do not worry about me. No one thinks I will be somebody one day, but I will show them. If you worry about anybody, worry about Betsy 'cause I'm worried about her ever being happy or rich. If you have any ideas on how to kids can make money please, please, please, let us know.

Sincerely,
James, your friend from Tumbleweed, Texas

Following the next Sunday at church, I wrote Oprah this letter:

Dear Oprah,

I hope the Big God don't punish me for stealing this paper and stamp. I know I should not steal, but there is a question making my belly hurt and giving me nightmares. Why sometimes I just stay awake trying to keep the bad dream from coming. I don't know anyone safe to ask but you 'cause I know you won't laugh at me or think I'm questioning God. I want to ask my Sunday school teacher, Mr. Boles, but he gets mad when I ask questions he can't answer. He thinks every hard question means I am questioning God. When he tells me to just shut up and mind my own business, I'm too scared to tell him I'm not questioning God. How did he ever learn anything? If I argued with him he'd call my dad, and he'd beat me again. Mr. Boles is funny and smart and makes us kids laugh, but I would not call him loving or kind. In fact, he can be as prickly as a porcupine at times. I think he's just mad 'cause he's losing his hair.

If you answer my question, I promise you I will hitchhike a ride to Chicago just to clean your bathroom for you. Cleaning the bathroom after my dad or his buddies throw up and shit all over the toilet and floor on Friday and Saturday nights is one way I can make my mama smile. It's hard to make my mama smile. My Aunt Nancy says I have sad eyes just like my mama's. I will do anything to make my mama smile. When my mama smiles, her eyes ain't sad no more. Do you think it's possible to have sad eyes with a smile on your face? But that isn't my real question. I ain't

75

got to it yet. I'm working up the courage to ask that one. Anyway, I can picture you walking in and saying, "James my bathroom ain't never been this clean, and the smell is like an autumn breeze." I saw that on a TV commercial right after your show one day. I don't remember what an autumn breeze smells like. Heck, I don't really even know exactly when autumn is, but I love the sound of those two words rolling off my tongue, plus I see orange and gold and red. I see you smiling and saying, "Why James, I bless the day I answered your question and you caught a ride to Chicago to clean my bathroom." Then I see you putting your hand on my head and messing up my hair and then blessing my heart. There's a warm tingle all over my body just thinking about it. I could make you smile too, Oprah, 'cause my aunt taught me how to clean a bathroom where everything shines and smells clean, not even like vinegar. I hate the smell of vinegar from the bottle, but after the smell goes away, it's the cleanest clean you ever seen or smelled. Aunt Luann says her Gramma says it kills germs too, and germs are one thing we can't see but hate anyway.

I know you have not answered my letters before so please don't get mad at me for writing you again. This is one I beg you to answer. I've never known anyone as smart as you. My classmates Alexander and Herkimer are the two smartest kids in our class and they are the teacher's pets, but I don't even think them two know the answer to this question. I saw Herk—that's his nickname—beat up a kid one day for stepping on his new shoes on accident. Herk may be smart, but he is not loving or kind. Ever since Betsy and I saw that we rhyme his name with jerk, and we don't care even if he is smart. We don't want glasses like his no more neither. Why, that very Friday afternoon then and there Betsy and I decided we like kind and loving people way more than smart people anyway, and we have not changed our minds ever since and probably never will. Anyway, you are the first person who is all three, smart, loving, and kind, that Betsy and I ever seen.

Now back to my question. There's a picture on the wall in the hall near my Sunday school room that scares me so bad I get nightmares, and there ain't no one but you I can ask. Just writing this down makes my hands tremble. Heck, I'm shaking all inside just thinking of it. Well, here goes the picture. Mr. Boles says that's the big God catching the saints, but he's letting the sinners fall into a dark wide pit with flames. Ever since my grandpa was buried in a deep, dark hole and I saw my dad burying LayDee one night in the dark, that picture at church gives me the willies. At least them holes I saw with my own eyes didn't have no flames dancing out of 'em.

Okay, my question is do you think any of them saints God is catching in his arms was ever called a sissy?

Sincerely,
James, your friend from Tumbleweed, Texas

PS: I just feel it in my bones that you will answer this one if you know the answer, and I think you do.

Late in the fifth grade at age twelve, an opportunity finally presented itself when I could have killed Harry once and for all—a way that was not even on my growing how-to list.

Harry returned home early one Saturday morning after an all-nighter at the local bar. During the prior weekend at the bar, a fight had broken out and a guy had hit him in the mouth with a crowbar. Harry's two front teeth were cracked during the brawl, and he was experiencing almost unbearable pain with those two teeth that were now badly infected.

He grabbed my mama's arm and forced a pair of rusty old pliers into her hand, demanding almost unintelligibly in his drunken stupor that she pull out both his front teeth or he would kill her. My mama fell limp to the ground, her full weight on her shoulder, pulling her arm out of the socket, and dislocating her shoulder. She cried out in excruciating pain.

Harry jerked her up under her arms like a rag doll, forced her up against the wall, put the heel of each of his hands on her shoulders, and pinned her against the wall with all his body strength as he gradually stepped back inch-by-inch. He got right in her face, spraying spit angrily into her nose, eyes, and mouth when his demands for her to stop screaming went unheeded.

Adam's baseball bat was standing by the door. I picked it up, top of the bat in my left hand, right hand on the end, and pushed in the back of his knees with the length of the bat. He just crumpled in on himself, landing in a pile, sitting on his heel, and falling face forward into the floor. He never knew what happened he was so drunk.

In a flash I retrieved the bat, ran to the kitchen, and hid it in a closet. As I walked back by, he raised one hand from the floor, grabbed me by an ankle, and tripped me down on the ground beside him.

I was so scared and angry about what he was doing to my mom and afraid of what he was about to do to me that I screamed I would gladly pull out his teeth. His anger moderated as I reached for the pliers, my hands shaking so badly I could hardly hold the handle. I clamped down as tight as my trembling hands would allow. I caught his right front tooth between the jaws.

My first grip was not strong enough, and the pliers slipped. I have never heard a louder scream from Harry before or since that bloody night.

I quickly picked up the pliers, knowing my life was hanging in the balance, and with all my might, I firmly planted first my right foot then the left, held the pliers in a deathlike grip around his left tooth, and the tooth came sliding out. I thought the roots would have been short, but they just kept coming and coming!

High from my success, I repeated the action with the second tooth that had to be rocked back and forth as I pulled down—eyes squinting—but both teeth were finally out, and my mom and I were still alive. Blood was spurting everywhere, and he and I were covered from head to toe. I grabbed a washcloth, stuffed it into his mouth, and screamed instinctively for him to bite down as hard as he could to stop the bleeding.

Dentistry was never on my list of possible careers after that night.

After all the hysteria subsided and I had the blood cleaned up off the floor, my mom had suddenly stopped screaming. Evidently, Harry had accidentally forced her shoulder back into the socket as he held her against the wall. I had nightmares for years from that trauma.

My deepest regret for years after that incident was that my instinct was to push in his knees and bring him to the ground, not hit him over the head with the bat and kill him instantly when he was about to kill my mom.

I had plotted for years on how to kill this lowlife who called himself a father, and I had missed the perfect opportunity! He was obviously intent on killing my mom for defying him by refusing to do what he was demanding her to do, and no one would have held me responsible if I had killed him. I sincerely believe, looking back, that I was convinced that he was invincible and I would have been the one dead instead.

Please leave him, Mom, I cry and scream.
We need a break from this bad dream.
At least fight back while you still can,
And stop this mean, abusive man.

My mama says God knows her plight,
And one day soon, he'll make things right.
Until that day, she prays each night,
We'll just survive the next bad fight

Chapter 8

Disney Delight

My favorite middle school teacher was Ms. Kiley. She loved poetry. The first day of school, she had written two poems on the blackboard. The first one said:

> I know how homely I are
> I ain't got no face like a star
> But I do not mind it
> Because I'm behind it
> It's the folks in the front get the jar.
>
> —Author Unknown

The class loved it. The second one said:

> I eat my peas with honey
> I've done it all my life
> It makes the peas taste funny
> But it keeps them on my knife.
>
> —Author Unknown

She told us that first day that she would be giving extra credit for any poem we brought to her. She taught us to see poetry in the world all around us.

She had the most beautiful silky red, sometimes curled hair, porcelain white skin, and gorgeous light blue eyes, and she smelled like the spring flowers blooming along the chain link fence on my walk home from school. She was a committed Christian, and the love just oozed from her pores. How I loved her!

She was someone I wished I could be just like. Her dress, shoes, and even slips were exactly the same color and shade. I wondered how she did that since her favorite colors were aqua, hot pink, and purple. The only slips I had ever seen were black or white. I wanted to ask her where she bought them but was afraid she would be offended if I did.

Her hair and makeup were always perfect, and she had a particular love for poetry. I learned many new words and concepts from her that have lasted me for life. I could not wait to get home one day and explain to my mom, using my index finger, counting the beats on all my fingers as we'd been taught, the concept of iambic pentameter. My mom listened closely, thrilled that I was thrilled, but she was clearly underwhelmed.

Ms. Kiley had had to take a medication as a teenager that stained and discolored her teeth, making them appear unconventional. The Jock Pack and other cruel guys called her mean names both in her hearing and behind her back.

Because she had also been teased and taunted all her life, she was acutely aware of the abuse I was enduring, having both seen it on the playground and heard it in the halls. She was painfully aware of my plight, although she was helpless to do anything much to help me at the time.

On several occasions she would often ask, when observing bruises or me limping or worse, if everything was okay with me while strongly suspecting that it wasn't. But because of my convincing lies back then, her hands were tied.

Years later she shared with me that she and some of the other teachers had gone to the principal on numerous occasions to see if anything could be done, to no avail. "Unless something is broken, or blood is spurting, there is nothing any of us can do," the principal would reply.

Ms. Kiley did not accept that nothing could be done. She moved my desk right next to hers where she could control any hateful comments from the bullies in the class.

Once when she overheard a bully whisper "faggot" at me under his breath, she went to the blackboard and wrote without saying a word:

> Bad things you say out of the blue
> Don't tell me about him—
> They tell me about you

Very soon after school started, she decided to start keeping me after school, allegedly to tutor me along with the other students who were having trouble in her class. But it was really to protect me from the bullies, who would be gone by the time she released me so she could be confident I could walk home or to work unmolested. She recently reminded me of an incident where I asked her one afternoon if she cared for me. She answered that shyly, saying yes, she cared for all of her students.

I then asked if she cared enough about me to give me two stamped envelopes for me to mail an already written letter to Oprah and one that I was waiting to write to her as soon as I got another stamped envelope. She answered that she was sorry, but she was not allowed to give her students any gifts according to school rules.

The next day, however, there were two empty stamped envelopes on the edge of her desk that she quietly and unobtrusively slid toward me with her beautiful long, pearl-white fingers outstretched, speaking volumes with her facial expression. My heart pounded out of my chest with excitement as I quietly put the long-coveted treasures in my notebook out of sight.

Being the loving person that she was, she would weave moral

lessons and principles seamlessly into her daily presentations, teaching us the importance of loving and caring for each other instead of harming one another.

One day as a class assignment, she asked our class to write an essay on what God looked like to each of us. She remembers that I responded quickly and loudly, without thinking, "My God is a chunky black woman!" The class burst into raucous laughter at my very serious referral to my beloved Oprah. I was crushed.

My poetry was very elementary, but buried not so far behind the words were the worries and questions that haunted me in my safe closet.

We had an assignment to write a limerick over the weekend about love, a favorite animal, or anything in nature like a tree, a meadow, the beach, or a mountain. I was always preoccupied with death, dying, bodies, cemeteries and epitaphs, and ghosts and was still grieving over LayDee, even though she had been dead over a year, I wrote a poem about her:

> Here lies the body of dear LayDee,
> Resting in peace underneath this tree.
> She was killed one night,
> Her death was a fright,
> But from brutal attacks she's now free.

Ms. Kiley would always lovingly correct my bad grammar that year. She would appropriately compliment whatever thought I would complete, and then she would say, "Now, try saying it this way …"

I will always be indebted to her, but grammar will always be a struggle for me. Since I was immersed in childhood in incorrect grammar, that's what still sounds correct to me after all these years of study. I would always do well on grammar tests, but then I would go back on autopilot to the way I had heard English from birth.

One afternoon after school that year Betsy and I were in a hurry to get to a favorite picnic table in the park to do some homework together. Betsy never saw the inside of my house until she and Adam started dating seriously many years later. I never, not once, had a friend over to my house because Harry would not allow it.

We decided to take a shortcut through an alley behind a strip center with a 7-Eleven, an optometrist's office, an Asian doughnut shop, a drycleaners, and a real estate office. We were arguing about a boy who had given Betsy a note telling her he liked her and wanted to "go" with her.

Unequivocally, I said, "Nope, I overheard him and some other guys talking filthy the other day about girls, a lot like Harry and his buddies do when he thinks we ain't listening, and you will not be his girlfriend."

As we reached the 7-Eleven, she was telling me in no uncertain terms to mind my own business, just as some of the older bullies were exiting with their expensive snacks and heard us arguing. They quickly emptied their hands, dropping their snacks behind a garbage can for later retrieval, and started running toward us. They were screaming, "We'll catch us some sissy ass and his mommy, and we'll fry 'em up for supper! Sissy croquettes, sissy croquettes," they chanted as they chased us.

Betsy and I started running as fast as we could, the bullies gaining on us as the flopping soles on the bottom of my secondhand tennis shoes slowed me down, stumbling on the rocky gravel. As we reached the end of the alley, the bullies gaining on us by the second, a cop car was sitting on the other side of the street, waiting to catch speeders on the perpendicular road.

At the first sight of the cop sitting there, the bullies came to a stop like roadrunners reaching the edge of a cliff in a cartoon, pivoted, and ran back the other direction, even faster than when they were chasing us. After only a few seconds, the cop turned on his lights and pulled forward into the intersection, turning right to chase down a speeder as he disappeared from sight.

As an adult, some of my best friends are law enforcement officers.

That was not the only time one possibly saved my life and/or limb(s) for just being at the right place at the right time. How I loved that officer that day. He never saw us, and I never even knew who he was.

When we got to the park, where a lot of people were playing with their kids, we unloaded our books on the picnic table and wrote a poem for Ms. Kiley's English class. The first two stanzas were from the good James for extra credit, and the second two were from my bad twin Jamal to hide safely in my journal:

If I had done something to you,
I'd understand why you are mad.
If I had stolen what was yours,
I'd give it back so you'd be glad.

If I had beat you in a race
With "First Place" written on the plaque,
I'd then know why you are mad at me
And I would gladly give it back.

Then from the evil Jamal:

I could have my cousin cut you up
In little pieces for the hogs,
Or I could unleash and sic on you
A pack of hungry, rabid dogs.

I would do the world a big favor,
With no feeling of pain or sorrow.
I would not flinch, I would not waver,
'Cause I could have less fear tomorrow.

As puberty became more and more obvious during the seventh grade, I had no one to ask what was happening to my body. Once again, I turned to Oprah.

Dear Oprah,

My body is changing, and I am scared. I think maybe it's cause of something I done. If my tits are sore and pooching out, does that mean I will soon be a girl? I will never take my clothes off in front of nobody ever again. Has this ever happened to anyone you ever knew of? I can't ever ask my mama 'cause my nosy brothers won't never ever let me be by myself with her, and if my dad overheard us talking, you can bet he'd sure give me a whoopin' if he found out my tits were pooching out, and my mama would just stand there and let him.

He'd say, "Okay, what you been doing you horny little bastard? I'll rearrange your face so no one will recognize you if you been doing what I think caused your tits to pooch out like that." Then he'd tell me take off all my clothes so he could see, and I would have to kill him somehow then and there. Then I would go to prison and help everyone there who had a mean dad. Then they would all like me. One good thing in prison, I would never go to bed hungry.

My friend says his mean dad called him a faggot and a maggot, and he asked me if I thought he should kill himself. I told him I'd miss him, but I understand why he's thinking about it. Do you have any idea of a painless way he could kill himself? Maybe you could do a show like that and help a lot of people. My friend is kind and smart, and he never did nothing bad to nobody I ever knew of. I want him to go peacefully in his sleep if he does it.

My dad's going around the house screaming looking for me. Gotta go. Please answer this letter. It's probably the most important question so far.

Sincerely,
James, your friend in Tumbleweed, Texas

PS: I will have to make this quick so I don't get caught.
The preacher at my church keeps talking about the
homosexuals. I just wish he would say what that
means. Do you know if it is something you are or
something you do? He says since Disney World lets
the gays come there, a Christian can't never go there.
I can't decide whether I want to be gay and go to
Disney World or not be gay and go to heaven until I
know what being gay means. How does my dad and
everyone but me know I'm gay? I thought about it all
night and decided if I can't go to heaven and be gay
and I find out I really am gay, I might as well just go
ahead and go to Disney World. I wouldn't know how
to get to neither one, so since I won't get to do neither
any time soon, I'll just be happy and try not to worry.
If I ever have kids, I'll just wait and take us all at the
same time and pray the gays or God don't do nothing
bad to us while we're there.

Sincerely,
James, your fan and friend in Tumbleweed, Texas

CHAPTER 9

CASKETS AND CHAOS

One day as I left junior high school walking home, the fields all around were full of brilliant royal blue wild bluebonnets, the Texas state flower, and Indian paintbrushes. The grass was just beginning to grow too tall. The sight of the overgrown grass proved to be a turning point in my life. I received courage in that moment because of the lack of food at home.

In that moment I started rehearsing what I would say to Mr. Pastore, the owner of the local funeral home (at the same time praying he would already be outside). I loved how he would greet me warmly and say, "Hello, son," as I passed by each time he saw me on my way home. How I longed for him to be my real father and me to be his real son.

Mr. Pastore was someone I had admired for a very long time. I was already in awe of the first dress tie I had seen on him years before. His starched white shirts with his initials monogrammed in script on the cuffs and crisply tailored dark pants with a single sharp crease running down the front screamed rich and successful to me. His pants cuffs fell perfectly on the tops of his flawlessly polished, matching wingtips with tassels. His cars were shiny silver limousines with never a spot of dust on them.

No matter what I'd been told to the contrary, my intuition told me that he was one rich man I could trust. When choosing hearsay over experience, I gradually learned to choose my own experience, especially if the hearsay came from Harry's lips.

As luck would have it, by the time I got to the funeral home, the sky had turned black, lightning was crashing everywhere, and rain was blowing me almost off of my feet. Just standing upright at my size was a physical feat. My blue sweat pants and faded lavender shirt were now soaked and sticking to my body. I ran under an awning that protected well-dressed mourners during these common storms in Texas that seem to appear out of nowhere.

This pouring rain gave me an excuse to linger near the door, praying that Mr. Pastore would soon appear. The pressure mounted because I knew I was on borrowed time, and even if I ran home like a track star, I was already in line for a beating. I didn't care. I hoped that either Harry would be gone when I got home or having to take cover for the storm would give me an acceptable excuse for being late.

In only a few seconds, the door opened and his wife, Mrs. Pastore, looked out to check the sky above to see if a tornado were about to hit. This was the first time I had met Mrs. Pastore. Even though I'd never heard the term *Southern belle*, that's what she was. She was a wonderfully kind woman who talked nonstop to anyone she ever met.

In true Texas style, she loved to tell stories and, as it turned out, was deathly afraid of being carried away in a tornado. As a break came in the storm, glancing intermittently toward the sky, she reported excitedly that almost fifty years ago to the day a tree had fallen over her grandmother's cellar door and trapped her grandparents, a girl cousin, and her in the cellar for several hours before neighbors came and rescued them.

Mrs. Pastore continued, saying, "As soon as we knew we were trapped, my grandmother, a seriously spiritual person, said cheerfully, 'Well, if God wants to come and get us in a tornado, that is just fine with me. Also, I cannot think of three people I'd rather go with.'"

Mrs. Pastore paused for a moment to catch her breath and refresh her memory, then continued her story. "Not missing a beat, my grandmother proceeded to use her kerosene lamp in the dark cellar to find some pickled peaches she had canned the previous August, knowing how much my cousin and I both loved them. As she opened them up, the aroma of cloves, ginger, and cinnamon filled the otherwise damp-smelling, musty air. My grandmother, God rest her soul, felt strongly that all negative emotions of fear, sadness, loss, and pain could surely at the least be lessened and often eliminated entirely with a favorite food."

With watering eyes, Mrs. Pastore paused and then continued. "We ate them right out of the jar, licking our fingers and laughing at our total lack of manners and decorum in our frightening predicament. I soon forgot how long we were trapped in that damp, musty-smelling cellar, but I have never forgotten the comforting feeling I felt that otherwise frightening day and why."

Tears filled Mrs. Pastore's eyes as she continued. "My cousin and I opened a jar of pickled peaches, ate them with our bare fingers, and smiled knowingly to each other at lunch after our grandmother's funeral years later. Pickled peaches have been a favorite of mine ever since that scary night," she said, fondly remembering what otherwise would be a troubling memory.

I don't know Mrs. Pastore's intentions that day, but her kind Southern demeanor and the result of her storytelling and the story's happy ending comforted and calmed us both down. Mrs. Pastore stopped and gazed again into the heavens, looking for a level bank of clouds signaling a tornado was developing, but also I really think she was looking up, imagining her grandmother looking down on her and reassuring her.

There was a deafening crack of thunder and lightning that seemed to land just beyond the covered porch, when she excitedly whisked me safely into the funeral home, grabbed an enormous thick, soft white towel, and wrapped me tightly to dry me out. I will never forget the comforting, clean, pure smell of that towel that was bigger, thicker, and softer than any hand-washed, fence-dried towel I had ever seen or felt.

Those towels Mrs. Pastore introduced me to that day bore no resemblance to the towels or rags I was used to. Mom usually washed all our clothes by hand, squeezing them out on a rub board and then draping them over the dilapidated chain link fence to dry. Many times I would rip a hole in a towel when attempting to dry my back. I would be red all over after drying off with those scratchy, hand-washed, fence-dried towels.

Mrs. Pastore's loving, tender, extra-long hug after tightly swaddling my rain-soaked body is something I've thought of often through the years. The entry in my journal that night read, "When you get rich, buy big, thick, soft towels with no holes in them. Also, send them to the same laundry Mrs. Pastore uses so they will smell just like the one she used on me today."

A year or so later I smiled when I heard Oprah Winfrey say on her program that the first things she bought with her first discretionary income were thick white towels.

Mr. Pastore stepped out of an office, bifocals down on his nose, nervously chewing on a pipe, carrying a handful of papers ready to be put into an envelope, addressed, and mailed to his accountant. He greeted me kindly with his usual, "Well hello there, son! All my life I've heard of high winds carrying things and people off, but I've never known of one carrying a fine young man like you directly to a funeral home door—while still alive!

"Why, I was just praying last night for God, if it were His will, to increase my business. I'm so relieved to see you are alive and not the answer to that prayer!" He had a big belly that bounced up and down while laughing at his own jokes.

I laughed nervously at his joke, distracted by my anxious thoughts. I was still agonizingly formulating how I would ask him for a job. I would have done anything for this secretly longed-for father.

After some fumbling of my words, I said, "Mr. Pastore, since I'm here, I was wondering if you would allow me to do odd jobs for you, like mowing the grounds, washing the hearses, sweeping and vacuuming the floors, and cleaning the restrooms."

As part of my verbal résumé, I told him that one of my many jobs at home was keeping the bathroom spotless.

What I knew, and he did not know, was that that chore was especially hard after one of Harry's weekend benders with several of his buddies at the house, so I had a lot of experience. I was anxious to prove to him my skills.

"You don't even have to pay me if you don't like my work. I will work for you for free," I heard myself foolishly say. What had I just said? There was no food at home after a long weekend binge where Harry had blown his entire rare odd-job paycheck buying rounds for the house at the local beer joint. We had nothing to eat, and I was offering to work for free? Confirmed fact: my mother had given birth to a sissy and a dummy. I was heartsick.

Mr. Pastore asked if I had a mower, and I responded, "Yes, but it's in the shop." I further embellished my answer saying that a part had been ordered, "But there is no guarantee when it will come in. If you have a mower I could use until it's repaired, I'll work even harder for you. Since I'm sure it is different from the one I have at home, you would need to show me how to use yours."

The truth? I had no lawnmower at home. We had no grass. I had never used a lawnmower. We only had stickers and weeds that had never been mowed. I was unwittingly mastering the skill of fabricating convincing lies so my audience, no matter how perspicacious, would not suspect I was lying.

Mr. Pastore was not a man to make quick decisions. He told me he would carefully consider my offer to help him and let me know his decision. Finally he told me one day about a month later when I saw him on my way home from school that he thought my idea was a good one. By that time I was in deep trouble at school for repeatedly going to sleep in class. My repeated protection patrols to check on Mom and the boys kept me sleep deprived. Sick at heart and thrilled beyond compare describe my conflicting emotions at his acceptance of my previously tendered offer.

I was alternately worried and excited. Harry had beaten me with his plastic belt (out of sight where the bruises wouldn't show) after the school called him and reported my malfeasance of sleeping in class. I was grieving inside. What would I tell Mr. Pastore? Harry had just grounded me for the entire summer for once again shaming and disgracing the family.

I was shaking all over by the time I got home. Harry was uncharacteristically kind when he learned that at age thirteen I would be earning a very generous amount of cash every week mowing and doing odd jobs around the funeral home full-time all summer.

He rescinded his earlier edict of grounding me, saying, "Your grounding was only for fun activities." The only fun activities we had were digging holes, catching tadpoles in the nearest storm sewer, and climbing trees with my brothers.

"A man needs a job, and a man needs to work. Now you go to work for Mr. Pastore, but whatever you do, do not disgrace this family." (That was code for: don't walk, talk, or act like a sissy.) For the first few weeks Mr. Pastore paid me in new, crisp twenty-dollar bills. Although I've made a very good living since, I've never felt richer than I felt that day, going from abject poverty and deprivation to twenty-dollar bills in my pocket.

Lying to Harry about how much money I was making never occurred to me because he had brainwashed me into thinking he was a member of both the KKK and the Aryan Brotherhood (another lie) and he had friends who would gladly punish me if he asked them to. So I proudly turned the cash over to Harry each week, first to protect my life, but also secretly hoping that somehow he would now be proud of me and could (and would) buy us more food.

Suddenly, instead of food or cheap beer, Harry had a growing liquor cabinet of Jack Daniels, Johnny Walker, Crown Royal, and Seagram's. He always told us they were gifts from some imaginary boss as a reward for his outstanding work.

My first promotion at the funeral home came after about a year and a half, but only after much begging and pleading to allow me to assist in the embalming room, instead of the menial chores I had been hired to do. For many weeks my pleas to Mr. Pastore fell on deaf ears. He argued that he did not think I was ready.

He never told me at that time why he felt I was not ready, and I never had the courage to outright ask him—probably because I was afraid of the answer. I just assumed he was the one who was not quite ready to expose me to the disturbing sights and smells of the embalming room, pick-ups at the medical examiner's office after autopsies, retrieving decomposed bodies in rivers, picking up remains in shallow graves that animals had dug up and partially eaten, and unattended deaths at home that had gone unreported for many days or even weeks.

His wife, Mrs. Pastore, on the other hand, was always a softy. Maybe she could intercede for me, I thought. After a long visit with her explaining how ready I was to graduate to embalming and going on first calls (picking up dead bodies), I overheard her say to Mr. Pastore, "Honey, why don't you just let him assist you on one case and see how he does?"

Finally one day when the time was right, Mr. Pastore had a serious talk with me about life and death. He described graphic situations that might come up and asked sternly, "Are you sure you are ready if these things, or God forbid, something worse, happens?" I assured him I was, but that moment did not come for several weeks.

Mr. Pastore loved to play pranks. This was also a way to test my readiness. While I was insisting that I was ready and not afraid of anything (those words did not match my insides), he told me firmly that a wealthy family was coming at 4:00 p.m. to pick out a casket for the husband and father.

As soon as I arrived at 3:00 p.m. after school, he asked me to go to the selection room, dust all the expensive wooden and metal caskets, wipe off any fingerprints, and vacuum any dust that might have gathered on the satin or velvet insides.

I was carefully rubbing down my favorite expensive, wooden cherry casket on the outside. I noticed the casket was slightly open because the interior lining was hanging out, a common occurrence when a casket was closed too quickly, but I went right on with my polishing, knowing I would soon be vacuuming the insides and would carefully put it back when I finished. I had never seen such beautiful, shiny wood. I could not believe I was actually being paid to polish it.

I was first visualizing the workers who had created this piece of art, wondering how much money they had been paid, how proud they were when it was finished, and wishing I could thank them in person. A picture of the wealthy person who would be buried in this expensive masterpiece appeared in my mind, as I wondered what kind of house he lived in and what he did to make him wealthy.

I could not wait to see his wife's reaction when she saw this exact model. I was convinced it was the one she would pick. I was sure she would be immaculately dressed, with expensive bag, shoes, and jewelry and perfectly coiffed hair. I was silently betting myself I could learn how to do the same kind of work he had done and do it as well or possibly even better when I grew up.

As soon as I finished polishing the outside, I started to open the lid, and up sat Mr. Pastore, laughing uproariously. I screamed and dropped my rag and polish as urine ran down my legs, bounced off my shoes, and puddled in a pool on the floor beneath me. Mr. Pastore never tired of telling that story to anyone who would listen. One of the last times I saw him in later years, we both laughed again at this prank.

Unexpectedly one day in the spring of 1996, Mr. Pastore hurriedly asked me to get in the passenger side of the hearse as I arrived after school. He had an apron and a white shirt waiting for me in the seat. I quickly changed clothes as we sped along. In a few minutes I would walk for the very first time into a hospital. As Mr. Pastore and I rolled the stretcher down to the basement where the morgue was located, my heart was pounding out of my chest, my knees were knocking, and my teeth were chattering. Mr. Pastore entered the code on the security plate and opened up the refrigerated area where the bodies were put immediately after death.

When he opened the door, my heart jumped into my throat, beating loudly. There lay a large man I knew, all but his face covered in a hospital gown and blanket. All the children in the community loved this man because he gave us all nickels and candy when he would see us.

The sadness gripped me like a boa constrictor and almost sucked the breath out of me. That was on the inside. On the outside, I was in my head, asking pertinent questions, assisting in a professional manner, and keeping my cool. Masking my fear of the unknown was something I realized later I had often practiced and was well on my way to mastering at age fourteen and a half.

This event was life changing for me. I had always been scared of the most benign bug, the faintest unfamiliar sound, or even a freaky Halloween mask. A strange feeling of freedom came over me as I faced my greatest fear and conquered it. Remembering this feeling of elation always reminds me of the gratitude I feel toward Mr. Pastore for mentoring and believing in me during this crucial period of my life.

Before I knew what I was doing, I told Mr. Pastore how kind this man had been to me. He responded, "This will not be the last person you will know when we get their body." Mr. Pastore could not say enough about how proud he was of me and how well I had handled myself during my first opportunity to learn the business. At that point, I did not believe him. His words contradicted those tirades of condemnation I had heard all my life and were now seared seemingly irreversibly into my psyche. These opposing concepts swirled in my head, at the least confusing me and at the worst depressing me.

Also, I was deathly (pun intended!) afraid Mr. Pastore might find out that I was just an undersized imposter, acting one way and feeling another. I knew he had the power to fire me any day, waking me up from the dream of becoming a funeral director and proving to Harry I would amount to something in spite of his constant predictions to the contrary.

Jake Kinshaw owned the local department store and was a good friend of Mr. Pastore. They had left for the military together, and their friendship was enduring and a delight to witness. One afternoon Mr. Pastore told me, "Tomorrow I want you to go see Mr. Kinshaw so he can fit you for a suit, shirt, tie, and dress shoes.

"Summer is almost here, and I could use a greeter to pass out memorial folders for the services." I was in my head, acting professional and grateful, but on the inside I was floating above the clouds.

Mr. Kinshaw was very friendly and outgoing, calling everyone in the town by their first name as he greeted them on the street. Mr. Kinshaw's wife, on the other hand, was serious, focused, quiet, introverted, and shy, with very little affect. I had never seen her smile.

She was the tailor at the store, and she had a reputation far and wide for her alteration abilities. Ministers and bankers came from all the surrounding counties, knowing when they left the store there was no way they could look any better. Mr. Pastore bought all the finest clothing for the funeral home. Often a family would bring clothes from home for their decedent to be dressed in, but more often than not, a family wanted to bury their loved one in brand-new clothes.

Because of my small size, I had to be carefully measured and the items had to be special ordered. It took several anxious weeks for the boxes to arrive. When they finally were delivered,

I immediately tried on the shiny black shoes that felt like velvet on my feet.

My toes did not have to be scrunched up, the soles didn't flap, and they fit like a glove. Mr. Pastore laughed and said, "I usually put my shoes on last, but you can do it however you like, son." I smiled, embarrassed by my naiveté.

Stepping nervously out of the shoes, I went into the dressing room and hurriedly pulled on the pants as my metamorphosis from toad to prince began. As each piece was taken from its package, unpinned, wrinkles shaken out, and slipped into the dressing room for me to put on, I knew any minute I would wake up from this dream.

Mrs. Kinshaw pinned up the hem on the pants, pulling and adjusting, stepping back and forth in front of and behind me, bending and stretching. She never said a word or even looked at me as she worked her magic, alternately squinting and opening her eyes widely, continuously frowning, straight pins held tightly in her lips.

Finally she stepped behind me to view both of us in the mirror. With a shocked look on her face, she could not help herself, and she smiled the first smile I had ever seen on her, before or after.

Whenever I hear the phrase, "A picture is worth a thousand words," the picture of her smiling face pops into my mind's eye. In that one magical moment, my dream to be someone Harry would be proud of was well on its way. There was just one problem with my dream. Many years passed before I sadly realized Harry hated me because of who and what I was, and nothing I *did* would ever change his opinion of me.

However, the die was cast. There was no turning back. I would attend mortuary school after high school. I would wear a suit like all the rich dignitaries I had seen come through the funeral home, mourning their equally rich friends and/or family members.

I felt nine feet tall. Even the KKK and the Aryan Brotherhood combined could not stop me now! If clothes really do make the man, every vile thing Harry had ever said about me would be proven wrong. I could be a pillar of the community working alongside lawyers, doctors, ministers, and teachers.

Almost simultaneously, Mr. Pastore gave me more and more responsibilities, and we both learned I had a knack for the science of preparing and mixing the embalming fluids. Amounts had to be accurately measured based on body size and weight, adding the perfect amount of color to the fluid based on the ethnicity of the decedent and on the discoloration of the skin caused by age and many diseases. At age fourteen, that soon became my job.

I also excelled at organizing the work area. Mr. Pastore knew exactly where he had last placed everything, but no one else could find anything after he touched it. I asked him on more than one occasion to let me organize the prep room, and he finally agreed I could start the project when business was slow.

Mr. Pastore went on an out-of-state death call. Business was slow, so while he was gone for an estimated twenty-four hours, I took everything off the shelves, out of the drawers, out of the closet, and out of the excess storage area. Working as quickly as I could, I separated the hair products from the chemicals, the cosmetics from the tools, and the various ragged magazines that cluttered the long wooden shelves, the tables, and the floors.

I clearly labeled everything and put it carefully back in easily accessible order. Mr. Pastore was an avid golfer and had magazines and books about golfing and years of funeral home trade journals, all commingled. Most of these magazines had corners of pages turned down marking an article or interesting fact.

After Mr. Pastore's parents both had died and after their house sold, he brought all their *National Geographic* magazines dating back to the '50s and threw them into the closet. I put all those various publications in individual stacks in dated order with the newest dates on top.

From that day forward, his wife, Mrs. Pastore, was my greatest advocate. She had tried for years to organize her husband, to no avail. That subject was the source of a great many arguments when Mr. Pastore would uncharacteristically raise his deep bass voice in anger at his beloved wife.

Mr. Pastore's eyesight was not as good as it once had been. He would miss spots of blood splattered on doors, on knobs, and down the otherwise spotless stainless steel legs of the equipment. Without saying a word, my personal mission became cleaning up those hard-to-see spots with my spray bottle of hydrogen peroxide. I don't ever remember having to be told once to clean a restroom. I loved cleaning the restrooms. Every time I cleaned one of them, I saw my mother's smile in my mind's eye.

By the time Mr. Pastore arrived back at the funeral home, the embalming/preparation room looked like a showplace. I must point out that keeping it that way became a constant and important part of my job. Chaos was definitely Mr. Pastore's default position.

He would often proudly walk back to the prep area after I had put in a hard day of cleaning, step back, and say, "We make a good team, son." I would smile to myself when I tried to identify in my mind the team role each of us had played.

After that weekend, *Mrs.* Pastore would regularly pull me aside and make confidential suggestions for me to follow and/or encourage Mr. Pastore to follow, since according to her, with Mr. Pastore I could do no wrong. She learned the hard way that she would only incite his ire if she interfered and told him herself.

I always knew I loved fixing hair, doing nails, and dressing up people. After all, I had been practicing for years on my mom during our playtimes. While I was assisting Mr. Pastore one day, cosmetizing a young black wreck victim, he was called away by an emergency phone call. When he returned after the call, his palms flew up to his mouth as he let out a gasp of sheer delight at my work. By the time I got to mortuary school years later, I was quickly put in charge of teaching the classes on this fine art. Mr. Pastore had been an excellent teacher.

We rarely ever had a black funeral, as the funeral business was and still is very segregated. The wreck victim was the son of one of Mr. Pastore's close friends from their military days. That was the first black person I had cosmetized, and I was very nervous about it. I kept thinking over and over, *What will I do if Mr. Pastore doesn't like it?* I had a terrible time going to sleep, thinking about how bad it could go wrong, and the next morning I wrote this letter to Oprah:

Dear Oprah,

I had a dream last night that I was getting ready to be you on your TV show. Your hair lady could not find a black curly wig to fit my little head. Every wig she put on me covered my entire face. You were watching her try and make me just like you from behind a curtain, and you were laughing so hard snot come out of your nose. Your hair lady asked, "Oprah, what are you doing hiding behind there? You are supposed to be on vacation getting some much-needed rest."

I told your hair lady, "I know what to do cause I've been fixing my mama's hair since I was little when she plays dead and lets me and my brothers play funeral with her." I took the big wig, put a wide rubber band around the middle part, and made a topknot with hair flowing down like water from my aunt's water sprinkler. It was so pretty! Then I took another rubber band, put it around the bottom of the wig, and pulled sprigs of hair over the band to hide it, and it fit perfectly on my head. Oprah, I'm as white as you are black, so that was another really big problem. I told them my friend Betsy says you look like a big melted Hershey bar to her, and I said just get a giant Hershey bar and cover my face. That makeup guy was amazed at how good it turned out. He said I could clean my face all by myself when we were through. They didn't let me walk out. They just put me on a board and carried me onto the stage and put me on a high stool on the stage behind a desk so no one could see the flopping sole on my tennis shoes. When the show started, I was shaking all over, but when it was over, all of them people come up to me and tell me it was the best Oprah show ever. They all wanted to know who did my hair so pretty. The show was about this one silly old woman who wrote and married all these bad men in jail, and I told her that one day she would be very, very sorry she was doing that. You winked at me from behind the curtain. When I woke up, I was wondering what a real Hershey bar tasted like.

Sincerely,
James, your friend from Tumbleweed, Texas

CHAPTER 10

COMING OF AGE

My mom's brother Bruce had been married briefly once, but that marriage did not last long. He lived in an old abandoned bus out on some acreage their older brother owned. He had no water or electricity. I always wondered how he lived without a water faucet. When our utilities would get cut off because of no money, I hated the water getting cut off the most.

We could live a long time without electricity, but lack of water sent me scrambling for ways to pay the bill as soon as I could not flush the commode or shower before going to bed.

Years later, when I'd embalm street people for county burials, their stench would remind me of Uncle Bruce. He cooked on a Coleman stove he'd found in the trash years before. "I never drank nasty tap water, no ways," he'd brag, laughing raucously. "Hain't got no kick."

He had a long, scruffy beard, and he stank all the time. His sour body odor mixed with the sickening smell of stale alcohol and cigarettes would gag me when I got too close. His too-big, frayed khaki pants were all greasy and dirty in the back and the front.

On the other hand, we kids loved his sense of humor. He made us laugh so hard over the silliest things. He spoke pig Latin, along with his own manufactured foreign language that had us all rolling on the floor when he would visit. I was always Amesjay and Adam was Damay.

In the summer of 1994, I had just turned twelve and Uncle Bruce, called Little Brother by Harry, was twenty-nine years old. One Sunday morning he was over at the house, drinking beer and shooting the breeze with Harry. Dad started screaming at my mom to bring them another beer. Mom could not hear Dad from the backyard. Dad's screaming got louder and louder.

When there was no response from the backyard, Dad got up angrily and looked out the kitchen window, where my mom was hanging wet clothes over the chain link fence out back. He forcefully banged the frame of the screen, knocking it off the hinges, leaving it barely hanging by a nail in the right-hand corner.

Things were escalating rapidly, and Uncle Bruce, afraid and probably knowing what was happening, started tickling us kids to lighten up the atmosphere. I was distracted and failed to protect my mom that day. I have never forgiven myself for my selfish neglect. That was another one of the several times Mom would come close to death.

We all instantly sobered up when Dad burst into the living room, carrying my Mom's tiny limp body in his arms, rushing toward the door, breathlessly screaming he was taking her to the ER because he said she had "slipped and fallen face first into the twisted metal on the top of the fence."

Her nose was stuck to one side with blood streaming onto her too-big, faded, hand-me-down multicolored flour sack dress, turning its front a bright crimson red. Uncle Bruce assured Dad he'd stay there with us until the church bus arrived or they returned. The church bus was on its way to pick us up for Sunday school.

Uncle Bruce reassured us that Mom would absolutely soon be like new and started nervously spinning yarns about several people he had known who had had that same exact accident and were now even better than they were before.

I doubted him because I had known him to lie before. I begged to stay home with him, first because Mom had washed all my underwear and I was waiting for them to dry, and second because the minute Dad brought Mom back home, I had to be there to see that she was all right.

Uncle Bruce said he was thrilled I wanted to stay with him because finally we could have some fun together without any interruptions. I was also thrilled because I knew that was something that would never have happened if Harry had been there. He would have insisted we all get on that bus so he and Uncle Bruce could have "a little peace and quiet for a change," and so they could talk about grownup things they wouldn't want us to hear.

After the bus arrived and picked up my brothers, Uncle Bruce feigned cheerfulness and proceeded to resume tickling me. We had had a particularly raucous time, laughing, punching, kicking, and rolling on the floor. The church bus arrived and picked up my brothers.

Our raucous play resumed until suddenly Uncle Bruce feigned great pain, saying I had kicked him in the groin. I quickly scrambled to my feet and rushed to him, worried about his safety, scared to death of what he would do to me to punish me. I knew with his size and girth there was no way I could get away from him. As he gradually caught his breath, he crawled onto the sofa, unzipped his pants, pulled out his oversized, engorged, erect penis, and said, "It'll be okay if you kiss it to make it better."

Fear gripped me like a large vise, but because I was so relieved I wasn't going to get beaten, I was facing him standing up in front of him, and leaned over trembling and kissed it lightly, holding my breath. He said, "Now put it gently in your mouth, because warm moisture will soothe it." I knew something was bad wrong, and I said, "I can't do that. It stinks."

He grabbed the top of my baggy sweat pants, pulled me roughly and angrily toward him, reached back and pulled the back of my sweats open, looked inside, and saw that I had on no underwear. His excitement visibly accelerated. His voice and facial expression changed as he pushed me back on my feet, saying scarily, "Well, ain't you the perfect little bitch? You've been thinking 'bout me and getting ready for me, too, huh?" He shoved me back to my feet. Standing in front of him, I was shaking and holding in the tears.

Already distraught about my mom and becoming increasingly distraught about my impending questionable doom, I collapsed my face into his chest, sobbing uncontrollably, screaming unintelligible pleas, knowing I was trapped and something terribly painful was about to happen to me.

My uncle's demeanor changed, his voice lowered to a comforting whisper, and he reassured me he wasn't going to hurt me. "Trust me, Bubba," he said. "I just want to show you a new manly trick that I promise you will like, not only now, but for the rest of your life. It's not just a trick for you. You can show all your little sissy boyfriends, and they will be your best friends for life." I had never had an ejaculation. As I neared a climax from his anal stroking, I started frantically screaming, "Help! Let me go! I gotta go to the bathroom!"

I was so terrified when I ejaculated. I thought I had urinated on myself. Uncle Bruce pulled his finger out, wiped it clean on his shirt, and pulled it from left to right across his neck, threatening to kill me if I told anybody. He got up and immediately left, leaving me alone and terrified. I wanted to talk with someone so badly, but I couldn't even question Oprah in a letter about what had just happened to me.

After that terrifying experience, I started bathing three times a day. I often got screamed at for taking too much time in the one bathroom we had and for wasting water. "Do you think we're made of money?" Harry would say.

No matter how many times I bathed for years, I could not fully get the greasy filth off my body or the smells out of my memory.

It is impossible for me to go to sleep to this day unless I've had a shower.

There were several more incidents with Uncle Bruce when all my efforts to try and make sure we were never alone failed. The wrestling in the third encounter was so violent I made sure I was never alone around him again. Looking back, I really think he and Harry plotted (and possibly bartered) to get the two of us together. I did, however, refuse to ever wrestle with him again, thinking it was my fault he had become aroused.

Later I remember I wanted to apologize to him for the shame I was feeling, and to reassure him I would never tell anyone our secret, but I would just freeze up and leave the room when he would come near me.

A few weeks later, he came up to me at a family funeral I was assisting. He whispered he wanted to tell me something he wanted me to be thinking about. He told me to stand back at the graveside because he wanted to tell me something. I resisted, but he took me by the shoulder and dragged me back beside him, a safe distance from the crowd.

"I'm going to tell you something I ain't never told nobody before, 'cause you've always been so special to me. Besides, this way you won't have to worry about gettin' some stupid girl pregnant, and it's so much more satisfying than some nasty ole bitch could ever be."

Uncle Bruce proceeded to tell me in vulgar detail what he had trained his buddy, Red, to do to him sexually, rewarding him with a cheap wine like Mad Dog 20/20. He laughed a vulgar laugh from deep within his body and continued. "A friend like Red won't never complain, turn you down, or make excuses why he don't want to do what you want him to do like ever old hag I was ever with.

"He don't want you to cuddle him after or tell him how wonderful he is, and you don't have to promise you'll never do it with nobody else. Nope, in fact, you can do it while he watches you without being jealous. Yep, little Bubba, you're gonna thank me long after I'm gone for giving you this valuable advice ain't nobody else in the world gonna give ya!"

"Oh, I gotta tell you right after you and I was together the other day," he continued as I tried to pull away, "I went home the next morning and thought back about our special time together." He leaned over and whispered, "Come over and I'll show you the streaks on the walls that didn't quite go the ceiling. It was so good that afterward I collapsed, went immediately to sleep on the bed, and didn't want none for another day or two."

As the crowd at the funeral began to break up, he looked at me, winked, got right in my face, and said, "Get somebody to bring you out to the farm one day, and you, me, and Red and them will have a party!" The thought of what he had been suggesting and the stinking clouds of breath covering me as he laughed turned my stomach.

The next time I saw him, he was a cadaver on an embalming table. The cause of death stated on his death certificate was alcohol poisoning. Mr. Pastore had no idea what this monster had done to me and kindly told me I didn't have to help embalm him if it would be too hard on me. I quickly assured him it would be an honor if he would let me. I do not recall the exact words I said, but I will always remember the cathartic release I felt after giving that monster a piece of my mind while embalming him.

Right after my uncle started molesting me at age twelve, violent sexual nightmares became another reason I could not go to sleep or stay asleep. I lived in fear that if anyone ever found out what I was seeing and doing in my sleep, I would be locked up and the key would be thrown away. Sometimes when I first woke up I wasn't sure if the nightmare was a dream or real. I knew I couldn't help it, but no one else would know it wasn't intentional.

These sexual nightmares never involved females like I would overhear the guys in gym class brag about. My nightmares always involved violent activities with multiple males holding me down, tying me up, and raping me one after another while they laughed and mocked me. I usually woke up from these nightmares, gasping for breath.

My prayer for God to take these thoughts and obsessions away from me was another unanswered prayer—until I became infatuated with a man nine years older than I was. When I fell in love with the idea of having a relationship with this handsome, financially successful man, the nightmares came less and less and were replaced more and more with pleasant wet dreams—and I didn't even know if this object of my secret affection knew I existed.

The grocery store was six or eight blocks from our house. My brothers and I would power walk with our mom to help her carry home the groceries. We were always in a hurry because if we took too long, our dad would accuse our mom once again of having an affair and us boys of helping to cover it up.

The manager was a handsome twenty-four-year-old Hispanic male with black hair, black eyes, and dark skin. He was six feet, two inches tall, 180 pounds, very fit and buff. I'd been seeing him for weeks and fantasizing about him, but I only looked at him when he was not looking at me. He was immaculately groomed, with creased khaki pants and a blue shirt with the store logo and his name, Ricky, embroidered above the left pocket.

One day in 1997 when I was fifteen, Mom, my brothers, and I literally ran to the store, and my mom sent me for staples on the other side of the store to save time. I hated going anywhere by myself for even a few seconds because I knew I was too small and too skinny to protect myself against anyone who figured out I was gay and decided to harm me.

Nervously and accidentally I turned down the wrong aisle and felt eyes watching me. I just knew someone had figured out I was gay or poor and was going to try to blame me for trying to steal something. As the footsteps got nearer and nearer, I turned around to see the store manager almost catching up to me.

He loudly said, "Stop, please, wait a minute." My heart flew into my throat, and I knew I was probably about to be accused of shoplifting or being up to no good. "I've been seeing you here in the store with your family for some time now, but it is very hard to catch you alone.

"I've just wanted to tell you I think you are cute, and I haven't been able to get you off my mind. You are someone I would like to get to know better. Here is my phone number. Please call me sometime." He shoved a card from the flower shop in the grocery store into my hand with his phone number on it and said, "May I hug you?"

A part of me did not want to hug him for fear he would feel my protruding ribs under my baggy sweatpants and oversized shirt, but another part of me was afraid this might be the only man who would ever want to hug me. He started hugging me, and I surprised myself when I gave in and I tightly hugged him back, trembling all over my body. He reached up with his left hand, took my right hand, slipped it between us onto his erect penis and whispered in a sexy voice, "See what you do to me?"

Confused, frightened, and trembling for the first time since the second grade, all the missing puzzle pieces fell into place, and life made sense. I didn't know why. I didn't know how. I just knew I was in love with this man and would do anything he asked me to do. Finally, this was a person who validated me and didn't want to hurt me. I wanted with all my heart to please him. I had no way at the time to differentiate between what was love and what was abuse.

I rushed to the other side of the store to hurry my mom so he would not see her bruises and question me about my home life. If he put two and two together, I knew there was a chance, based on Harry's threats through the years, that he or any adult who found out would report her condition to the authorities and take us kids away from her.

I was also ashamed and terrified he would see we were using

paper vouchers from the Love Center to pay for the groceries. Luckily he was nowhere in sight when we checked out and quickly left the store.

I started sneaking down to my aunt and uncle's house late at night to use their phone to call Ricky after my aunt and uncle went to bed early. Uncle Jim had to get up at 4:30 a.m. Both my aunt and uncle were deep sleepers, and Uncle Jim could not sleep without the radio loudly blaring by his bedside.

I would walk quietly in the back door, use the phone in the den where Aunt Rosie's TV was blaring, and talk freely with Ricky during his favorite TV show, *The Golden Girls*. We would have a running commentary on every outfit they wore, whether Dorothy was really a lesbian or not, and if Betty White was truly that naive a person.

During commercials and slow plot developments, we discussed my trips to wrecks and river bottoms picking up dead bodies. Ricky would talk about a fake "slip and fall" accident that day or some prominent person who was arrested for shoplifting. He was a great storyteller, and I had to be careful not to laugh too loudly.

Ricky kept pressing me more and more to sneak out and meet him somewhere. During our late-night phone conversations, he started talking about all the pleasurable things we could do to each other. Afraid, I made excuses and kept putting him off.

Harry had his bluff in on me. Looking back, I realize I was also afraid of what would happen, not having had any real sexual education of any kind other than Uncle Eugene's pornography, Uncle Bruce's molestation, and witnessing Anna and Harry's tryst. Each of those incidents had left me with more questions than straightforward, honest information. Deep inside, I knew I did not know what he would want me to do, and I didn't want to be belittled for my naiveté.

Finally one day I agreed to meet him at a local pizza place. I asked my aunt to take me there to apply for a job and leave me to take a test. I told her I would walk home.

She sweetly agreed. That was my first visit to a pizza restaurant. Pizza has never tasted that good before or since. Ricky was so nice looking, worldly wise, and amazingly kind and loving (at first) to a naïve, emotionally deprived fifteen-year-old that my attraction to him was irresistible.

CHAPTER 11

BUSTED AND BANISHED

Journaling was an escape, as well as being therapeutic for me. Before I met Ricky at the grocery store, I had had a crush on one of my classmates but had no idea how (or whether) to let him know. I poured my heart out to my journal and thought I had the journal well hidden. Weeks after I met Ricky, Harry found the journal, snooping in my room.

That evening, physically and emotionally exhausted from work, where I had been helping a hysterical couple pick out a casket for a three-year-old son they had just lost to drowning, I walked up on the front lawn, where all of my worldly possessions were hurled all over the front yard. Valuable papers and schoolwork were shredded like confetti.

Harry, I soon learned, had found the notebook, which had fallen on the floor behind my bed. The notes about the boy at school were months old, so I was startled and puzzled when I saw Harry standing in the window, peeking out from behind the shade, with a look of demon possession on his face.

He lunged out the front door and off the dilapidated porch with the unmistakable intent to kill all over his face. He stumbled as he stepped off the porch onto a pile of round beer bottles, sliding into the weeds in the front yard, coming to a stop in a bed of thorny weeds and stickers. He began screaming in pain with his injured knee and bleeding torso.

Through his screams of pain, he was yelling that I no longer belonged to this family. I was a disgrace, and I should just be glad he could not get up because there would be no more lessons for me to learn if he could. He said my mom was a whore who had fucked her dad and enjoyed it, so there was no telling who my real dad was.

He screamed at the top of his lungs, "There's no way I'd have had a faggot for a son." Once again he resorted to his favorite taunt of rhyming faggot with maggot. He shouted he knew when he caught me at three years old wearing my mom's hand-me-down high heels from the Love Center, putting on the makeup she used to cover her bruises, holding a broken hammer handle for a microphone, and pretending to be Tina Turner on TV that she was the one who made me gay by not putting a stop to that.

Used to Harry's frequent weekend binges and the attendant circumstances, consequences, and raised voices, the next-door neighbor came running out, knelt down beside Harry to assess the severity of his injuries, and went back inside to call an ambulance. Crying hysterically, I gathered up my belongings and headed for my Aunt Rosie and Uncle Jim's house, where I lived for about a year.

Instead of turning my weekly income over to Harry, I started sending it to my mother by my aunt. I felt such guilt and shame because I thought I was abandoning her and my brothers, and I could not deprive them of life's necessities. Although I was deeply hurt that my mother was obeying Harry in not having a relationship with me, I still felt financially responsible for my brothers and for her.

My first inevitable (and predictable) mutual sexual encounter happened on a weekend while my aunt and uncle were out of town. Ricky came over, and we started drinking, doing drugs, and smoking. Ricky smoked pot, but pot made me sick and nauseous. We had sex, and he teased and mocked me for weeks because I had said, "What do you want me to do?"

My cousin walked in on Ricky and me, not in the act, but cuddling each other in the nude afterward. She screamed to high heaven and ran straight to my parents' house and told Mom. Harry had been missing for two days.

My mom came running down the street to my aunt and uncle's house, already distraught about Harry's disappearance. Almost unintelligibly through gut-wrenching sobs and cries, she said, "James, how could you do this to me?"

The irony of that comment stunned me. I'd had that first initial thought about her behavior so many times. Then I had a moment of sudden clarity. Since my actions were clearly not anything I was doing to her, maybe her actions were not something she was doing to me.

That first sexual encounter with Ricky was extremely painful, but he was very gentle with me. I fell more and more in love with him, and for me at age fifteen, I was sure this was who my life partner would be.

When Harry eventually returned home and learned my cousin had caught Ricky and me in the nude, he reportedly built a fire and burned my baby and school pictures, including any picture that had me in it.

He burned or threw out everything I had ever touched in my life "to kill all the AIDS germs!" All my worldly treasures disappeared, adding one more reason to kill Harry. I was barred from seeing my brothers because "we have to protect them from this pervert," a cousin reported Harry as saying.

I had one picture that was taken when I was six years old in my journal that was still hidden behind the sheetrock, the picture hidden safely in my journal, and that's the only remaining picture of me from my childhood.

When my aunt and uncle returned from the weekend and my cousin told them I had had sex with Ricky while they were gone, they told me to take everything I owned and move out.

Since Harry had abandoned my mom and me when she found

out she was pregnant with me and had turned down their offer to adopt me, Uncle Jim and Aunt Rosie were not really on speaking terms with Harry. They had no regular communication, and I'm sure my mom had never told anyone why Harry kicked me out of the house.

Small towns often have strange unspoken rules. So often the things you want them to talk about, they keep secret, and the secrets you want them to keep to themselves, they tell anyone who will listen. Maybe it was denial, but I'm sure no one in the family talked about my attraction to the same sex in any explicit way. "Unless I see it with my own eyes, it ain't true, and I don't have to deal with it," ruled the day in these types of situations that people did not want to or did not know how to handle.

I immediately moved to another married cousin's house. Both Mae and her husband, Leon, were the party-hearty type, addicted to drugs, alcohol, and anything that could be smoked in a pipe. That's when my nonstop drug and alcohol abuse began.

I had no restrictions on my behavior. Ricky was welcome to come and go as he pleased, and there were no questions about what I was doing, where I was going, or when I did or did not come home.

Up until that time, I had been so tightly controlled and frightened by Harry and his threats that this instant freedom was something I did not handle well. In fact, I dropped off the deep end.

Betsy and I started experimenting with alcohol and more exotic drugs and going to gay clubs. Although I spent much of that time hugging a commode, I went from being a caged bird to flying, not with the eagles but with the vultures, leading directly to my eventually dropping out of high school altogether.

After about five months dating Ricky, he gradually started becoming an increasingly angry person. He was insanely jealous of my relationship with Betsy and even accused us of having an affair. The physical abuse—constantly being slapped and knocked around—started gradually but quickly escalated into full-blown physical and verbal fights.

Once again I was either hiding my bruises or lying about how I got them. During one sober moment, I remember thinking that I was back with Harry! How well I had learned from my mom how to protect the perpetrators in my life at all costs.

Betsy, her girlfriend Cassidy, Ricky, and I were having a ball dancing, laughing, and drinking at a gay bar one evening. Out of the blue, Ricky flirtingly motioned with his index finger for me to go with him to the restroom. We went in the stall, and he picked me up by my collar and neck. He was almost twice my size in height and strength, and he started choking me. I could feel the life leaving my body along with the oxygen.

I knew I was going to die. When we were gone too long, as I was struggling not to pass out, Betsy burst into the men's restroom, pushed her way into the stall, and started beating on Ricky and screaming for him to let me go. She rescued me, and after several years I was convinced she had saved my life one more time.

Proverbs 26:17 was one of Mr. Pastore's favorite quotes when an altercation would break out among family members when a loved one would die and another relative would get between them to break them up. "He that passeth by and meddleth with strife not belonging to him, is like one that taketh a dog by the ears."

The scene in the restroom that scary night was a perfect example of that proverb. When I finally got my breath after Ricky dropped me in the stall to free his hands to protect himself against Betsy's hysterical pummeling, I started raging at *her* for not minding her own business. *I* could have easily choked *her*! Betsy often reminded me through the years that I had raged at her but said absolutely nothing to Ricky, who, there was no doubt, was trying his best to kill me.

I immediately thought back to the incident with Anna, Harry, and Mom where Mom said nothing to Harry but was willing and ready to murder Anna. I finally learned the lesson not to get between an alcoholic and his booze and never to get between two people who are each other's drug of choice.

Dear Oprah,

I seen your show on suicide and decided I didn't want to die and stopped myself from taking a bunch of pills so I could just go to sleep and not feel my pain any longer. I'm so sorry now that I won't be able to see your show any more 'cause I've now decided living ain't worth the cost. When you get this letter, I will be dead. Harry has hated me since I was born. Mom loves Harry more than anything and will not go against his orders not to see me or he will kill us both. Mom says she loves me too much to make Harry kill us so she just stays quiet. My aunt and uncle kicked me out of their house cause of love, and Mae and Leon, my cousins, ain't never home. They are always out working in the day and drinking and drugging every night. I'm so sorry for all the trouble I've been to everyone. Please tell them if they ask you.

Sincerely,
James, your friend and fan in Tumbleweed, Texas

I never mailed that letter to Oprah because the next day she had a show on suicide with a devastated mother begging anyone thinking about suicide to please consider what it would do to his or her mother. It was months before the thought crossed my mind again.

CHAPTER 12

R.I.P.

James Byrd Jr.
5/2/49—6/7/98

Matthew Shepard
12/1/76—10/12/98

Betsy's promise in kindergarten to protect me forever from the bullies was a two-edged sword. I would often get mad—I now know from the realization and embarrassment that I could not protect myself—when she would step in and stand up for me. What I now know is that I would have been dead without her help, especially during high school and the following several years.

In the tenth grade, in October of 1998 as a freshman in high school after I had turned sixteen in May, Betsy and several other girlfriends ran up to me, excitedly telling me about the annual bonfire that was to be held on the following Friday night. Most of them had gone the previous year with some of their older friends and had been talking for a year about the fun they had had.

I immediately responded, "I don't want to go. I feel uncomfortable just thinking about it." My friend Chassity—nicknamed Butch—said, "Come on, James, ain't nothing gonna happen. Why you be so scared all the time?"

I quickly replied, "I ain't scared. I just don't feel up to going."

Each of these friends had the gift of persuasion that a seasoned courtroom attorney would have been envious to claim as her own. They didn't take my no as an answer, so I continued lying as convincingly as I knew how. "No really, I may have to help out at the funeral home. If I go to the bonfire, I may miss a call, and I really need the extra money to save up for college."

I wasn't actually able to save any money for college because I needed all of the money I could possibly earn to get utilities turned back on, buy food, get medicines for Mom, and buy clothes for my brothers so they wouldn't be picked on.

"Nothing will happen. We'll have fun. Come on, James, don't be a spoil sport," bombarded me from all sides. This was not the first time I would go against my gut feeling, wanting so desperately to be loved by my peers.

The bonfire was many acres behind the school building on adjacent unimproved property the school owned for later expansion. It had been raining for several days. Betsy drove her Geo Metro, splashing through the potholes in the ground, as we stuck our heads out the open windows, hollering as loud as we could, dodging the muddy spray. I thought to myself, *This is more fun than any old bonfire could ever be.* I reluctantly exited her vehicle when we arrived at the site, feeling in my bones the fun had come to a stop for me.

While at the bonfire site, I started noticing several of the Jock Pack whispering and laughing to each other as they got closer and closer behind me. There was a lot of confusing noise and commotion around the increasing fire, and because of my being several inches shorter than everyone in the crowd, I suddenly realized I was apart from my group.

Several boys surrounded me, carried me off by my four limbs, dropped me from about three feet in the air onto the muddy ground, formed a circle around me, and beat me almost unconscious.

I remember lying on the ground, holding my breath, and staying still in hopes they would think I was dead, get scared, and run off. They stood around plotting. "Let's do the world a favor and get rid of one more bastard queer tonight." I slightly opened one eye to see if I could run.

I lay there thinking, *Where are my friends? Why aren't they helping me? Who's going to look after my mom and brothers? What did I ever do to any of these people to cause them to treat me this way?*

The why of their heinous actions suddenly became immaterial as I realized if I were going to live, I had to run as fast as my legs and flopping shoes would allow. I started running, and they started chasing me again. I heard a bottle hit the back of my head, but I didn't feel anything when it hit me. The running back on the school football team caught up with me and tackled me.

In the back of all pickups in the country in Texas is a rope used to rope cattle, drag logs and brush, secure large loads in the pickup bed, and pull other trucks or dead animals out of a ditch or mud hole. An excuse in the South for not being able to attend some function is to say, "I'm sorry I can't go. I've got an ox in the ditch." Without a strong hemp rope, there is no way any animal could easily be pulled out of a ditch.

Everyone started tying me up with a rope around my ankles, and as a blow smashed directly on my nose, I lost consciousness. In and out of consciousness, I watched the boys wrap the rope around my ankles and slip it back underneath itself, forming a slipknot. As long as there is pressure on the rope, it is tight and secure. When pressure is released, the knot releases. I knew if I could release the pressure, the knot would release.

When I regained consciousness, I had been tied to the hitch behind a 1990 rusty light blue Ford F150 single-cab truck. The blast of the exhaust was sucking the breath out of me, and I knew my life was about to end.

The boys inside the truck and in the bed of the truck were laughing, howling, and throwing their hats up in the air, shouting at the tops of their lungs, "Another faggot bites the dust! Yeehaw, motherfuckers! Let's do this! Head for Uncle Bubba's farm. He's got an old abandoned well with a concrete lid, and that's where we'll dump what's left of him."

They started torqueing the tires on the muddy ground, driving and pulling me behind the truck. I tried grabbing the rope to loosen the strain and release it but could neither reach nor pull myself up to where it was tied, and pulling on the rope only made the knot tighter. The water standing in the holes along with the mud luckily provided some relief to the abrasions to my buttocks and back.

Miraculously, the truck slowed down, bumping over some deep potholes full of water from all the prior rain. The right front tire sank into a muddy, water-filled hole, and the truck came to a stop with the front tire spinning. Everyone jumped out of the cab and over the edge of the truck bed and flew toward the stuck front tire. Instinctively, I edged my body toward the trailer hitch to loosen the rope and kicked my feet into the air, and the knot released.

At that moment, with super strength, I pulled on the knots where they were slipped in on themselves around my ankles, much like untying a shoe. I released the knot to get the rope off of my right foot, and in the pulling and releasing of pressure, the rope untied from the ball of the truck hitch. I jerked the rope off of my ankles and took off running. I remember running as fast and as hard as I could to escape. That's the last thing I remember until I woke up with my mom crying over me on the front porch. Neither one of us had any idea how I ended up on that porch.

"I'm sorry! This is my fault! Who did this to you?" I didn't want my mom seeing me like this. I didn't want to hurt her. I told her I was fine as she tended to my mud- covered body and clothes, the mud mixing with blood from the cuts and wounds.

By this time my nose was swelled to twice its size. She begged for me to let her call the police, but I persuaded her not tell anyone, much less the police. What I knew that she did not know was that two of the kids had dads in law enforcement.

I told my mom that the boys would be taken away. "If we call the police, they will call Child Protective Services (CPS), who will come to the house, see you have no food, and take Adam and Joseph away … and if Dad finds out when he comes home, he will hurt all of us!" There was no way I could see that we would be better off by calling the police. We would lose either way if our secret got out. Letting my secret out also meant my shame about the incident would become the subject of public ridicule.

I stayed there Saturday and Sunday recovering from the incident. I thanked my lucky stars that Harry was away on a bender and I managed to avoid him completely all weekend.

I owed my life that night to an older man named Claud Wallace who was a retired veteran of World War II. His job as an enlisted man was to secure cargo on a navy vessel. From as early an age as I can remember, he sat out in front of the grocery store each Saturday and made balloon animals, showed us kids magic tricks, and most importantly taught us how to tie and untie knots while our parents were in the store buying groceries. Everyone in town affectionately called him Pops.

I loved the knot he called a bowline on a bight, mainly because it was the hardest to learn. Some of the kids, especially the bullies, never were able to learn it because the intricate procedure was so confusing to them they just gave up trying.

I learned it immediately. Finally there was something I could do better than they. Second, this knot untied very easily, but the harder you pulled on it, the more secure it became.

As Pops used his string to teach us, he would tell us stories about the war. He was an admirer of President Truman, who he was 100 percent sure saved many American lives. Pops' regiment was about to invade Japan when President Truman dropped the bomb on Nagasaki and Hiroshima. That very quickly led to the end of the war and Pops' release from the military.

Because President Truman had saved Pops' life generations ago, I am 100 percent sure Pops' teaching me how to tie that knot saved my life that night behind the truck. If I had been the one tying the knots on those monsters, instead of the other way around, those macho boys would never have gotten loose from that trailer hitch.

CHAPTER 13

ACADEMIC APPRAISAL

I went back to school that following Monday. When I got off the school bus, my furious girlfriends were waiting to scold me for sneaking away from them before the bonfire got started. They were only furious until they saw me.

Nancy saw me first and with hands covering her mouth screeched, "Oh my God, James!"

They were all talking over each other when I just calmly interrupted. "I was in a car accident. The car was totaled, but I lived, and I will be okay."

Butch replied, "Bullshit. I know what happened, James. I overheard the boys talking; I thought they were just full of bull crap, but I believe it now. I'm calling the cops!"

I pleaded with her not to, and she agreed she wouldn't if I would tell her "the truth, the whole truth, and nothing but the truth."

I finally said, "Okay! Yes, Butch! They did it! It was my fault, though! I caused it!" (I had learned well from my mom that victims are always at fault.) I told her all the gruesome details, and she reluctantly agreed to keep what happened a deep, dark secret.

Carlotta felt so ashamed because she wasn't there to protect me. I told her, "It's not your fault! It happened; I'm alive! I'll be okay!" I continued saying, "I just want to graduate and leave this town! I will. I will get away. I have to be better. I have a goal in life, and I'll reach that goal. I just have to deal with the madness until I graduate."

Carlotta grabbed me and hugged me, telling me she loved me and that I was like a brother to her. She said, "Please, James, get out of here; go somewhere else. Don't you have family you can go stay with away from this godforsaken place?"

At that moment I did not want her love or sympathy or advice. I disputed all she had just told me, telling her my opposing opinion of myself. "You are so wrong about yourself, James!" she exclaimed, stopping me before I was through denigrating myself.

"Stop it," she cried. "You're a beautiful, warm, caring person that deserves *nothing* but the best that life has to offer." I couldn't help but cry. I told her that I felt as if I had nobody to trust, talk to, or be honest with.

After that emotional exchange, she said through her tears, "I want you to know something about me and what's happened in my life that I have never been able to tell anyone else." She continued to sadly relate that some of the same abuse that had happened to me had happened to her. Sworn to secrecy, we are both protecting perpetrators in her life to this day.

A national tragedy had occurred in June when James Byrd Jr., a black man, was dragged to his death behind a pickup in Jasper, Texas, in June of 1998, not because he was a gay person but because he was black. That was clearly a racial incident.

What I wouldn't let myself think about was that the perpetrators sounded so much like the Jock Pack. I was still scared enough over that incident, knowing it had also almost happened to me for a different reason.

About a month later, the class was given an assignment on public speaking and was instructed to draw inspiration from current events in the daily newspaper. I had never really read a newspaper in depth until this class. My experience with newspapers were the articles my cousin Blake brought to me prior to this time containing reports on local petty crimes we were involved in, but only we knew who the delinquents were.

"Public speaking is the world's number one fear," my teacher Mrs. Ryan explained, "and practice in that skill will serve you well for the rest of your lives." Our assignment was to read an article in the paper each night, come to school, and put it in our own words in front of the class.

I would get my cousin Mae's newspaper in the evening and read her daily paper to prepare for the next day's class. The first paper I read had the headline, "The Murder of Matthew Shepard." As I read the article, my blood froze in my veins. It became clear to me that I could never go anywhere alone ever again. The same cowardly perpetrators of the dragging event were not only after the blacks but also the gays. They preyed on the outcasts, the poor, and the vulnerable.

The fears of the relatively small things in life that I had experienced as long as I could remember suddenly clearly were insignificant. I did not use that article for my homework because several in the Jock Pack were in my class and I was terrified of giving them any ideas. Another startling and life-changing realization came over me after the dragging incident. For the first time in my life, I now knew I could die.

At a particularly low time, all the secrets, shame, and fear were getting to be more than I could bear. I wrote a note apologizing for all the trouble I had been to everyone. I poured out my heart on paper, and then I took an overdose of my cousin's meds. I woke up in the hospital with my stomach being pumped. I was furious! I was such a failure that I could not even kill myself.

After mandatory counseling for a short time, I returned to school to even greater threats and taunting. The first afternoon back to school, Nancy and her friend Tara, a senior, had an idea. Tara was one of the best catches in school (and the only girl in school who was shorter and looked younger than I). She had just broken up with her boyfriend right after buying a gorgeous dress for the prom.

Nancy said, "Look, James. Please don't be offended, but the reason the guys in the Jock Pack are hassling you is because they think you are gay. Life is a game of chess. These guys are outmaneuvering you at every play. We have got to start making better moves, honey. Those fools think you are the queen, and we have an idea of how to turn you into the king and bumfuzzle them all. Before you say no, please just think about it.

"Tara has broken up with Beau, as the whole school knows, and she needs a date to the prom. She wants to invite you to take her, and she will lavish you with affection during the event. She will pay for everything because she's inviting you and it will be a big favor to her as well. What do you say?"

After some thought I said, "Okay. I will go, but I will pay for my tux and our tickets. If I'm going to be a king, I better start acting like one. That's the only way I will agree to it."

We both had the time of our lives because we were just close friends who genuinely loved one another. The Jock Pack backed off of their taunting for several weeks, wondering how in the world I got that beautiful girl to go with me. Maybe they had been wrong about me after all, a friend told me she overheard them saying. For a short time the taunting stopped as the Jock Pack tried to figure out why or how they could have been so wrong.

I punished myself unmercifully, however, because I had saved out money from my paycheck to rent a tux. I grieved over what my mom and brothers had had to do without because of that decision. That short respite from the taunting was almost worth it, and it gave me an idea I shared with my friend Betsy.

Damon (Demon) was walking toward us after school, and I asked Betsy to show affection toward me when the guys were around. That only worked well for a very short time until we'd start to laugh at the awkwardness of the exercise or until they finally learned that Betsy really was just my friend and that my brother Adam was the one she was falling in love with.

My sobriety lasted a very short time. The partying in

combination with drug and alcohol abuse continued, and I am thankful that I survived that period. In retrospect I realize that the pain and discomfort of a queasy stomach saved me from disaster on more than one occasion.

When I was sober, I felt more female than male. All my life at social gatherings, dinners on the ground, or potlucks at church—as we refer to them in the South—I would notice that the males were huddled together talking (interspersed with raucous laughter) about sports, the latest cars, hunting, fishing, women's body parts, and the guys' latest sexual conquests (or plans for near future conquests).

At that point in such gatherings, growing bored by the male bragging, I would soon be the only male surrounded by female friends and/or relatives of all ages talking about decorating, fashion, and the latest recipes that tasted just like their calorie-laden counterparts but were low in fat, sugar free, and could be consumed in unlimited quantities with no fear of weight gain. I learned very early that being a thin female meant being pretty, attractive, and desirable.

A mostly unspoken question on heterosexual men's minds in such gatherings was why any man would *choose* to lower himself from the higher, loftier, preferred social status of male to the subjugated lower class of female. The answer to that mostly subliminal why question in every male's mind was easy for me to also answer without the slightest equivocation in my own mind.

Being overwhelmingly female in a male body was never a *choice* I made, just as I never *chose* the all-male participants in my dreams that began at about age eleven and continue to this day. It was that simple.

I can choose to eat chowder or stew.
I can choose to wear purple or blue.
I can choose my ties.
I can't choose my eyes.
I can't choose an attraction to you.

One morning as I woke up in a strange motel room soon after moving in with Mae and Leon, I could only remember walking into a gay bar the night before with several girlfriends, ordering a drink, and meeting the type of cute, buff guy I was usually attracted to. That was the last thing I remembered. My head was pounding with a pain I had never felt before as I slowly opened one eye that morning after.

There was a light streaming in from behind the blinds, lighting up the three lines in the corner where the two walls and the ceiling met. Those three lines became six, then nine, followed by vomit that rolled out of the side of my mouth as I turned my head to the right, leaned over the edge of the bed, and made a fresh deposit into a layer of previously partially dried vomit on the floor beside the bed.

Terrified, I rolled back gently to the left and shrieked as I saw an older, strange, naked man lying on his back with a hairy chest and potbelly, arms raised above his head. The back of his head was cradled in the palms of his hands. His smelly, hairy armpits and a straggly beard with quarter-inch grey and black spikes of hair growing out of his chin and cheeks gagged me all over again.

As my muffled gagging roused him from his deep sleep, he grunted, gradually dragging his grimy fingernails through his hair and scratching his scalp. He lowered his arms and folded his hands on top of the four gold necklaces buried in his chest hairs like snakes hibernating in the weeds. He had a huge, gaudy class ring on the third finger of his right hand and a gold band on the same finger of his left hand. On his right pinky finger was a gold ring with the initials AJ.

The fatty flesh bulged on both sides of all three rings, almost covering the smaller pinky ring. I remember thinking that those rings would have to be cut off when he died, they were so tight. He had obviously gained a lot of weight since originally putting the rings on his once slimmer fingers. His wedding band was a horrid joke. I had also, just seconds before, begun the process in my mind of ordering an extra-large casket from the catalogue to handle his enormous frame.

I learned the hard way that buff young heterosexual guys would work their way through the university by hustling young men for older, horny, unattractive men with cash.

The pimps, for lack of a better word, would greet a young man cheerfully soon after he walked in the door of a gay bar, take his drink order, bring the drink he had ordered laced with a pill or powder, or French kiss him with a pill on his tongue he pushed into the victim's mouth, dance with him seductively, arouse him sexually, and then in a carefully orchestrated amount of time to allow the drug to take effect, turn him over to the older guy for money.

The speed with which the pimp would unzip his pocket in his expensive jacket, stuff the cash inside the pocket, close the zipper, and then sprint to the front entrance to replicate the con rivaled that of an Olympic track star. This type of business venture on Friday, Saturday, and Sunday nights paid off many student loans. Or better still, it avoided having to take out a student loan at all, in many cases.

One night I don't remember how Betsy, Butch, and I got to a party at a lake house. I later decided I had ecstasy placed in my drink by a one of the guys at the club. I fell in love with a fluffy white carpet in front of the fireplace. I started screaming at an imaginary guy to stop staring at me. I urinated on a potted plant I thought was a urinal.

I soon learned when living with Mae and Leon that according to addicts, there is no serious partying without alcohol, drugs, and/ or sex. The mind has to be altered to have what addicts consider real fun. My need to belong was getting harder and harder to satisfy, making me more and more vulnerable to mind-altering substances and the activities that would follow, with the added benefit of being unencumbered by pangs of conscience.

When I was sober, I wanted to be faithful to a loyal life partner and have children, a home, a good education, a good job, and a purpose to my life. I wanted my partner to be mine alone and for me to be his alone. When in a mind-altered state, just like an alcoholic with alcohol, one sexual partner for me was too many and a thousand was not enough.

As soon as a drug would take effect, I felt pretty, desirable, loved, and cherished. Everyone loved me, and I loved everyone. The sky had never been so blue. The drapes were the most beautiful shade of crimson I had ever seen. There was not one ugly person in the room. Those mornings after, however, gave new meaning to a rude awakening.

I am grateful that Mr. Pastore never confronted me about my drug use. Maybe he didn't want to know, or maybe he just didn't want to acknowledge that it was happening. Because of my job, I stayed sober most of the time I was around him. I loved him too much to disappoint him.

I'd had enough. I was done with school. I walked to Mae and Leon's house from school one day, crying about the injustice of it all. I'd had a lifetime of torment that had to stop if I were going to survive.

Betsy kept begging me to come back, but I knew in my heart that was not going to happen. The temporary desire to escape all the bullying and abuse—just to ensure my survival—sadly became greater than my lifelong mission to prove Harry wrong.

After I quit school, I decided there was no God. He had made me defective and had never come to my aid when I prayed. He was too remote, too, to be of any benefit to me. It did not matter one bit to me how the universe appeared into being or who was responsible for that plan. The big bang theory made as much sense to me as the "Big God" theory.

The conclusion I reached was that God damned anyone wearing the title that any evil bully decided to give him. I felt like a square peg in a round hole spiritually without knowing why. That god had never been and would never be a friend of mine.

Off and on I would halfheartedly study for the GED, usually at slow periods alone at the funeral home when my work was done, but my partying kept getting in the way. It was getting harder and harder for me to work, study, be alert, and be motivated in all areas of my life. I would buckle down and study for a few days, only to go wild the next weekend. On more than one occasion, I lamented once and for all that Harry was right and I would never amount to anything—just like he always told me.

One Friday afternoon while partying with a bunch of friends, once again I was whining and moaning that I would never be able to pass the GED. I was destined to be just like Harry, with no education, I raved on to any friend who would listen, and with no opportunity to be anything but a minimum wage worker, barely getting by.

My friend Butch was standing up against the wall in her skin-tight, heavily starched Wranglers and Western shirt with white pearl button snaps, under which she wore a tightly wrapped Ace bandage to hide her boobs.

Nobody messed with Butch. She was stronger than most of the boys, and she would whip your ass with very little provocation. I was no exception to that unspoken rule. Her right leg was bent into a V shape, right hip resting on the heel of her boot propped against the wall.

Her right hand was in her right pocket. She held a Styrofoam cup in her left hand. She spit tobacco juice into the cup when it became clear she had heard enough. After hearing enough of my complaining that day, she angrily jerked her right hand out of her pocket and wiped her mouth from her wrist to the end of her thumb, shouting, "Bitch, I am so sick of that broken record you keep playing. Frankly, that pity party you cherish so much is making me sick."

One of her friends was going the next day to take his GED, and she called him and got the phone number to sign up.

She dialed the number and handed the phone to me. "Either

do something about it, or stop fucking talking 'bout it," she said as she handed the phone to me. "Just take the goddamned test and then you will know how hard it is, and you will at least be better able to study for it. I've never known anyone to pass it the first time anyway."

I learned that there was a waiting list, but if I would show up a few minutes before 9:00 a.m. the next day, I could get a spot if there were any no-shows.

Nancy, Betsy, Butch, and I arrived several minutes before 9:00 a.m., but by the time we got to the head of the line, the lady told me that there had been no-shows, but it was too late because it was after 9:00 a.m. I started crying, begging, and pleading with her to reconsider since the test had not actually started, and because I had been in line since way before 9:00. She called the supervisor over and whispered with him, and he said, "Okay." My friend handed them her mother's credit card that she had preapproved for a loan, and I sat down.

I was still wired from the party the night before. I was wide-awake, focused, and determined. It was a four-hour test, and I finished in less than three hours. I walked out to the car where my friends were waiting for me, and told them elatedly that I had passed.

Since we already knew that the results would not be mailed for a week to ten days, they laughed and taunted me, saying, "No, you probably didn't pass. Stop it. You will be too depressed if you don't. You are still high, and there's no way you could have passed."

When the results arrived in the mail, my friends hid them from me until they all started screaming that yes, I had passed! I could not believe my ears. My dream of going to mortuary school was becoming a reality. Ecstasy, not from a pill, is the only word that describes my feelings at that moment.

I had already confidently started the process of applying to mortuary school because I was sure I had passed the moment I had finished it. I immediately called the kind lady who had been processing my application. She told me I had been approved, but I would need to apply for financial aid.

I called my old counselor from high school. He had been relentless in begging me to come back to school, to no avail. He had been a true friend to me, and he told me to come by his house after he got home from school, and he'd help me with the application.

We spent less than an hour filling out the application, and he faxed it to my new friend at the mortuary school. She called back and told me she had completed her portion of the form and that I had been approved for financial aid. *Could this really be happening to me?* I thought. *I'm actually going to become a funeral director just like Mr. Pastore.*

Chapter 14

Saying Good-Bye

I woke up early the next morning and literally ran to the funeral home. I ran in screaming and shouting, showing the letter proudly to Mr. Pastore. He asked me where my car was, and I told him it had died again (Mr. Pastore had helped me buy an old car from one of his widowed friends a year before, but it had given me a lot of trouble and was always on the blink.)

He asked how I was going to move to Dallas, a three-hour drive, to go to school. I told him that my friend Betsy was going to drive me with only my clothes. He excitedly invited me to go in his car for a Coke "to celebrate your amazing accomplishments." He told me years later that he had been worried I would never achieve my goal of becoming a funeral director after I dropped out of school.

We laughed and cried over our Cokes and my certificate as we shared in the joy of my acceptance into mortuary school. I thanked him for having faith in me and giving me a chance to have a job and help my mother and brothers out financially. I told him I wanted to be just like him now, a respected funeral director. I promised him I would also mentor young people who needed someone to guide, teach, and believe in them.

Mr. Pastore got a death call but demanded I meet him at the funeral home the next morning no later than 7:30 a.m. The thought never occurred to me to fail to do anything he told me to do. He was more than my boss and mentor. He was my kind, loving surrogate father and beloved teacher of life lessons.

I met Mr. Pastore at the funeral home at 7:20. As I pulled in, my car started to overheat, spewing steam three feet into the air. Mr. Pastore raised his voice and said, "Son, hang that car up!"

"Why won't you just let me buy it from you?" he asked, with his unlit cherry-flavored tobacco filled pipe held between his teeth. I shyly explained to Mr. Pastore that this was my very first car, and I wanted to keep it more than anything.

That day was the twenty-eighth day of the month, and Mr. Pastore had just read his Proverb verse of the day, Proverbs 28:27: "He that giveth unto the poor shall not lack; but he that hideth his eyes shall have many a curse." He said, "There are organizations that benefit the poor with donated automobiles, and yours would be a great gift to give them," he continued, "but that, of course, is completely up to you."

With conflicting emotions, trusting Mr. Pastore completely, but also knowing that car would never survive a trip to Dallas, I went to the glove box, took out the title that was already in his name, and handed it to him, smiling, along with the key. Once again he said two things I loved to hear from him in one short sentence: "Son, bless your heart."

He stuck his hand in his pocket, removed his lighter, lit his pipe, sucked on it to ignite it, exhaled sweet smelling smoke into the air, and said, "Son, hop in my Suburban over there, and let's take a ride."

I loved the aroma of the sweet-smelling cherry tobacco that permeated the air and seats in his shiny silver Suburban. Asking me to go with him to town was not unusual. I had no idea where we were going or what he had in mind.

We drove straight to the automobile dealership in town, where a salesman showed us several vehicles lined up in a row. I knew Mr. Pastore had already been there looking at new Suburbans for the funeral home the afternoon before.

While he was looking at the new Suburbans, I went straight to a new white Chevy S10 pickup strategically parked at the front of the building. As I stood there, Mr. Pastore walked over from the Suburban he had been looking at and said, "Now this is what you need to take all your stuff to Dallas, but it's also one that will be affordable on gas."

Did I hear what I think I just heard? Stunned, I said, "Yes, sir. In a couple of years I will be able to buy one just like this when I finish school and get a job." He laughed his infectious belly laugh and said, "Get your skinny ass in the driver's seat and tell me what you think!"

I got in, and my face lit up in amazement! Mr. Pastore waited only a split second, raised his voice, and said, "Well son, what the hell do you think about it?"

I said quietly and formally, my voice audibly shaking, "Well sir, it's too pretty! It's way too nice for me!"

He gently grabbed my elbow, shook it, and stated, "Oh bullshit! It can't be too good for you when you're the owner." His words did not register. I quickly got out of the truck in disbelief.

He yelled (screaming sounds too effeminate for Mr. Pastore, in my humble opinion at the time) a little louder, making sure my hearing was okay, "Well, did you hear me, son? The truck is yours! I want you to be able to attend mortuary school feeling good about yourself. When you get there it's a tough school. You cannot be worried about whether your vehicle will start each morning and get you there, and you will never pass if you can't get to your classes and get there on time every day."

I looked at him and stated in disbelief, "Nuh-uh. This is not true!"

He laughed and pulled me close to his body to give me a hug and said, "Son, you deserve it!" I was in shock. I had never heard these words in that order in my whole life. His hug in that moment was as emotionally satisfying as the pickup was physically satisfying.

The gentleman who helped me sign the papers was a short man with brown hair gelled very closely to his head. He was slender and wore a blue dress shirt with a black vest and a very colorful red, black, brown, and blue bowtie. He wore dark brown pants and brown shoes with tassels on them. *He is very rich*, I thought. *How else could he afford such nice clothing?*

He whispered as I was signing the papers, "You sure do have a nice dad!"

I did not disagree or correct him as I smiled and responded, "You ain't telling me nothing I don't already know, sir!"

As the keys were placed in my hand, Mr. Pastore said, "Son, I'm very proud of you! There's just one stipulation. When you get there, you have to promise to keep in touch with me to allow me to know you are well and safe. If you need anything, please let me know. I'll always be here for you!"

We had a ritual I didn't understand until that day. He did it again. He pointed to my chest saying, "What is this?" I looked down as usual, as he moved his finger to raise my chin and hit the tip of my nose when he said, "Son, you're still way too gullible." This time I finally got it. The next time, I would know not look at my chest just because he told me to!

He pushed the keys into my hand. I started crying, and he said firmly, "Okay, son, stop that crying shit," as he pulled me in for a last father-son type hug. As we parted, I saw his tear-filled eyes. I sat for several seconds with my head on the steering wheel, sobbing uncontrollably.

As Mr. Pastore and I parted ways, I noticed an envelope on the passenger seat with, "SON" scribbled on the front. As I sat at the red light on Main Street, I opened the envelope, and ten crisp hundred-dollar bills stood up inside with a note that read:

Son:

No matter the distance, no matter the obstacles, *you* are going to succeed! *You* blessed my life from the day you asked me for a job. I have seen you grow and mature into who *you* are, and I see what you'll soon be. *You* have made me see life in a new light, as *you* have brought joy, excitement, promise, and life back into my home, my business, and my marriage. *You* soon will see yourself in the way my wife and I see *you* as a special, unique person, and a true light to all who meet *you*. Please always remember how special *you* are no matter what. When *you* feel lost, call me anytime. Hang in there and make yourself as proud as we have always been of *you*.

Oh, and stop crying; you're messing up this happy moment.

I laughed as I wiped the tears he predicted ahead of time would come and continued reading:

See, laughing is better, son! Be courageous and know that you will make as great a difference in the lives of Dallasites as you have made in ours. Be true to yourself, and show the world who the real James Mercer is!

Love,
Mr. Pastore

In that moment, as I drove my new truck to say good-bye to all my family, I chose to believe that a higher power would see to it that Mr. Pastore never lacked for anything. At the same time, I promised that same higher power that I would never close my eyes to the poor.

The first stop on my good-bye tour was at cousin Mae and Leon's house, higher than any liquid or pill had ever taken me. At first she and her husband thought it was one of my tall tales, but when I showed them the paperwork, they were as amazed as I. I thanked them for being there for me and opening their home up to me when I was as low as a human could get. We all cried and hugged good-bye.

I stopped by Uncle Jim's house, thinking since I was leaving he would have a change of heart. When I arrived at the door, I heard the key click locked, and they pretended they were not home. I could see through a crack in the curtain that they were inside, pretending to be gone. The only two vehicles they owned, a maroon Crown Victoria and a two-toned blue Chevrolet show truck, sat in the driveway.

The shame washed over me like a tsunami, but I got up the courage to raise my voice anyway. "I'm leaving for Dallas tomorrow for mortuary school. I just wanted to say I love you, I thank you for everything, and I just wanted to say good-bye." There was still an eerie silence inside the house. I left, feeling rejection, disappointment, and shame.

As I drove down the street sobbing, I knew I had to at least see if my mother would let me tell her good-bye. The trembling inside me first started when I rounded the corner and saw the house, then moved to the outside of me as I walked through the weeds up to the door.

My mother opened the rusty screen door with Harry standing behind her. She automatically moved toward the screen door and peeked around me to get a full view of my new truck. When I told her Mr. Pastore had bought it for me, she meekly commented under her breath what a blessing Mr. Pastore had always been to our entire family.

She then broke down sobbing, begging me not to go. Harry interrupted her pleadings with his hand protecting the latch above the screen door, while pulling her back roughly by her shoulder toward him and away from the door.

His comments were predictable. He seamlessly played the disgrace card, the accepting handouts card, and then angrily interrupted me when I told my mother, while completely ignoring him, that I was leaving for mortuary school with a pithy two sentences: "Good riddance. Nobody cares about you leaving, so just stay gone forever, and leave your mama alone; you have caused enough damage."

My instinct was to do exactly the opposite of what he was ordering me to do, but I knew there was no way I could get my mom away from Harry, and my decision to go to school would ultimately be the only way I could take care of her like I had always wanted to. I prayed the day would come when she would be proud of me.

Although I left Mom's house with a heavy heart, I started counting all my blessings. What a privilege it had been to know Mr. Pastore. I decided the only way I could ever pay him back was to model myself after his example.

I promised myself I would be a good man like Mr. Pastore, always telling the truth to the best of my ability no matter how bad it hurt me. I promised I would intercede for the poor, abandoned, and/or abused, helping to change their lives forever for the good.

I also promised myself I would keep my eyes open for the next James—a young person to mentor the way I had been mentored. Helping another struggling young person was the best way I could see of honoring all of the things Mr. Pastore had done for me.

I promised I would also love and protect innocent animals just like Mr. Pastore. He often brought his border collie, Bradley (his wife's maiden name), with him, especially at night when he would be alone in the funeral home or doing removals from a home or nursing home.

How he loved that dog! Mrs. Pastore would often jokingly comment that she wanted to come back after her death as either Mr. Pastore's pickup or as his cherished dog Bradley.

CHAPTER 15

MORTUARY MATTERS

The campus of the Dallas Institute of Funeral Service Mortuary Schools (DIFS) was located in an older part of Dallas, Texas, an approximate three-hour drive away from Tumbleweed. Mr. Pastore had always driven on the occasions we were required by state law to take bodies from unattended deaths to the medical examiner's office there for autopsies, but I had never stayed in or driven in a big city before.

The two-day orientation for the semester started on a Thursday. I left very early that morning to make sure I was on time. I was two hours early, and the parking lot was empty. Even though the locked glove compartment safely held the envelope with ten crisp hundred-dollar bills in it, I had no idea how far that would go toward rent, clothing, gas, and food, so any use of it had to be for absolute necessities.

The teachers rotated for the task of teaching the orientation class each semester. Ms. Campbell taught us that semester, and I knew that first day she would be my favorite teacher. To myself, I called her my Dallas Oprah.

All the professors seated us in rows arranged alphabetically, and in every class my chair was in a middle row right in front of the podium where the teachers stood to teach. The first day in Ms. Campbell's class I fell in love with her. She had a gorgeous face, amazing teeth, and a beautiful smile. She reminded me of a tiny Oprah—a single, loving, smart, intuitive, wild, and crazy black woman with an electrifying sense of style and grace.

She would enter from the right side of the room where the door was, and while running on her tiptoes up the aisle, she would mimic Edith Bunker's high-pitched voice. "Well, Ahchie, I'm back! Did you miss me," she would ask me as she reached the front of the room, turning to face me in the front row. The class would laugh hysterically. This morning exercise was like a bugle call that woke us up and put our minds on alert. I made all As in her class.

She would bring homemade snacks to class and say as she handed them to me, "You first, Ahchie, take all you want, then pass them around." How did she know I was always really, really hungry—surviving on Ramen noodles and peanut butter?

She was always happy and upbeat. She was another example in a long line of pure-hearted, kind black people who were the complete opposites of how Harry had portrayed all black people to me.

She tutored me, encouraged me, and counseled me. And without her conducting the orientation and her subsequent friendship, I could have easily been another dropout statistic. I will always be indebted to her. She means the world to me.

I remember when she came in one day and announced that she had married a minister and we were to call her Mrs. Allen from then on. Out of habit and disappointment, feigning a poor memory, I would continue to call her Ms. Campbell. No matter who this man was, and I never met him, I knew in my heart he was not good enough for my beloved Ms. Campbell.

I was devastated during orientation when I learned that we would be required to wear a suit, white shirt, and tie every day. The only suit that belonged to me was the one Mr. Pastore had bought for me two years prior. It had been very well taken care of, going to the cleaners after each service, but I knew I would have to buy another suit, another white shirt, and another tie. That meant I could not sleep in my suit in my car each night.

We were told during orientation that we would be required to start looking and acting like licensed funeral directors so it would be second nature when we received our associate's degree. There were many reasons sleeping in my truck was my only safe and sensible option the night after the first day of orientation. Too many unanswered questions (with no one to ask) about this unknown adventure bombarded me.

What does a motel room look like inside? How much of my money would it take? Would I be too small and young looking to rent a room by myself? Would the owner ask where my parents were or if I were a runaway? Would the owner have a key and come in and molest me if I were ever able to go to sleep? Would anyone inside know I was gay, what would they think about it, and what would they think they could do to me without retribution because of that assumption … and on and on?

I calculated that I could almost buy a new suit with the same amount of money for two nights' rental posted on the outside of several motels I drove by.

Harry's sister lived one and a half hours away from Dallas and had told me I could stay with her and her husband until I got established. I drove to my aunt's house for the weekend after the two-day orientation, worried that I had made a bad decision about going to school. Rent was too high in Dallas, based on what several students told me they had learned.

Mrs. Petty, one of the teachers at the mortuary school, asked me on the following Tuesday morning where I was staying. She had come to work at 4:30 a.m. to work on a deadline that was due before class started at 7:00 a.m. and had seen me sleeping in my truck in the parking lot. I had decided to save the gas money to my aunt's house the night before.

She warned me that the neighborhood was too dangerous for me to sleep in my truck. I told her tearfully that I was poor, had a limited amount of money that had to last me until no telling when, and had not been able to find an affordable place yet.

Later in the morning, the dean of the school, accompanied by Mrs. Petty, called me aside and told me I had come to school prematurely and that I needed to work really hard for a year and save so I could come back with enough money to survive.

Who did he think he was, giving me that harsh advice? I protested loudly and angrily, stating firmly that coming to this school had been a dream of mine since age thirteen. I told him I already knew how to do everything because I'd been working at a funeral home for years.

All I needed was the degree from his school, I continued without catching my breath, and no matter what he had just said, going home was not an option. What I knew, that he did not know, was that Harry could not be proven right. His prediction that I would never amount to anything and should already be dead with AIDS anyway was a lie, and I was determined to prove it.

Mrs. Petty sent me to class, and then caught me in the hall. She told me she had been touched by my passion and impressed by my spunk and whispered that I could rent an extra bedroom from her for much less than an apartment would cost if I liked.

Thanks to my stash from Mr. Pastore, I had enough money for my first month's rent. With the nagging and fearful question of my rent settled, I was able to go buy another suit, shirt, and ties.

Mrs. Petty had rented another spare bedroom to a classmate who had started school three months earlier. Brittany became my close friend and knew the ropes. She was a great resource and source of comfort to me in those early scary days and homesick nights.

Instead of belittling me when she heard me crying in my room the second or third night, she quietly knocked, came in, and shared that she had cried the first month she was there as well.

She saw how lonely I was and asked if I would let her introduce me to another classmate who had started school at the same time she had. She thought Asa could be another person to help me get started and be a good help and friendly companion to me. I thanked her but turned her down. I told her I was putting all I had into study and had neither the interest nor the effort to spare to put into a relationship.

Because of her kindness, I became more vulnerable than I really wanted to and opened up to her that I was also afraid to have a relationship with another male because of all the grief that had caused me in the past in my little town even before my first sexual experience.

Brittany raised her voice and said, "Honey! This is not some small town where everybody knows everybody's business. This is Dallas, Texas. First of all, there are so many people that it's impossible to know everybody's business. In the second place, please trust me when I tell you that, for the most part, everybody's too busy minding their own business to worry a whit about yours."

I listened skeptically, sitting on the side of the bed, with elbows on thighs, hands on each side of my head, thumbs under my ears, with my eyes pointed to the floor. She continued, "I'm not saying some ignorant ole biddy in Walmart might not walk on another aisle to avoid you, or some kid worried about his own sexuality might not say something under his breath as he passes you. Immature, ignorant, uninformed people are everywhere, and you cannot fix them. They have to want to fix themselves, and that's something you cannot control. Just remember: any awful things they say or do are about them and not about you!"

(I smiled as I thought back about almost the exact same quote Ms. Kiley had put on the blackboard in the seventh grade.)

She took a deep breath, carefully weighing her next words. "How do I say it? Please, don't take this wrong, but it's a lot about how you conduct yourself. I've noticed you don't make eye contact with people. You hold your head down, looking at the ground most of the time.

"Have you ever found that hundred-dollar bill you act like

you're looking for?" We both laughed. I realized I was not crying anymore. "Stop acting and looking down," she continued. "You're asking people to keep you down when you are already acting down. It's not all their fault."

I loved how she worded that. In the kindest of ways, she was telling me I was a contributor. Anyone I had ever known before in my life would have said, "It's all your fault." I was beginning to think Brittany was someone I could trust.

"Now, hold your head up and look me in the eye," she said firmly. I slowly obeyed. "Now stand up." I stood up, and she stood up, and we faced each other. I slowly looked up at her face. I had never really seen her. She was about five foot nine, with gorgeous shiny black hair and bright blue eyes. We started laughing when she said, "Now, was that so hard? No!

"Let's have an experiment at school tomorrow," she continued. "Get your head out of your ass and your eyes off the ground. I can guarantee you that you will not miss any hundred-dollar bills if you do what I say. Look up and smile at people. Be friendly—but not too friendly—you know, like you are just glad to see each person."

Was the God I didn't believe in putting all these strong women in my life, or was it accidental that I would run into them everywhere I went? That night I nicknamed my new friend Brittany "my Dallas Betsy." That was the last time I cried because of homesickness.

What I didn't tell her that night was that all of my relationships had taken too much of a toll on me physically, emotionally, and psychologically. At first, a love interest would be gentle and loving, only soon to turn around, almost always because of jealousy, and control and abuse me. The first sign the relationship was deteriorating was almost always verbal, and then the verbal abuse almost always escalated into physical abuse.

I had promised myself, driving to school in my new pickup that first Thursday, that when I started school there would be no more drinking, drugging, partying, or staying up too late. I had to succeed in school. That was not negotiable. I had been praying for this since my early teens, and I could not blow this opportunity. I had too much to prove to too many people, but especially to Harry.

The next day at a break between classes, Brittany walked up with this guy I just assumed was her boyfriend. She greeted me sweetly, then proceeded to say, "Asa, I want you to meet James. James, meet Asa."

With all the grit I could muster in my body, I raised my head, looked him straight in his gorgeous dark brown, almost black eyes, shot out my hand to shake his hand, and said genuinely, bordering on formally, "I'm *so* glad to meet you."

I put a slight extra emphasis on the *so* since Brittany was watching. Asa greeted me back genuinely and said, "I love your new truck. I wanted a truck so bad, but I had to take my mom's car she gave to me when she bought a new one." *Good*, I thought to myself, *he has no clue that I've been poor all my life.*

Honestly, I could have killed Brittany in that moment. *Why doesn't anyone take me at my word?* I thought to myself. *What gives this person I've just met the right to meddle in my business and push me into things I don't want to do?* I had to smile inside, though, when I realized that this encounter only confirmed my nickname for Brittany. All the feelings our new friendship conjured up, both positive and negative, were certainly familiar ones.

I had seen Asa before in school. He was not my type. I had always been attracted to the "bad boy," dangerous type. He wore a goatee, and I had never dated anyone with facial hair. He was a little pudgy, and my boyfriends had always been buff, with large pecs—the type who goes to the gym every night after school or work.

So when he said, "What do you like to eat?" I said, "Mostly salads," because I noticed that most wealthy people I knew were stuck on salads. I was terrified that anyone I met would know by even the slightest outward sign that I had come from a poor family.

He said, "Great, I hate eating alone. We'll go get a quick salad after school today."

He had told me, not asked me. It worked. I also felt comfortable with his choice of the word *quick*. I thought, *I'll just go with him this one time and send him packing, explaining to him kindly about my commitment to myself to study hard and not get embroiled in a complicated relationship.*

Asa was a born salesman but not the back slapping, too friendly type of salesman who visited too loudly with strangers in an elevator and turned everyone off. He was smooth, low key, and genuine. There was not a fake bone in his body. He did not ask me for a date. He never asked me any question that could be answered yes or no.

He always asked open-ended questions that required a lengthy answer. Before I knew it, we were walking into a restaurant called the Garden Inn. He had picked it, thinking it was obvious by its very name that it would have salads. He could not have been more wrong. It was a Chinese buffet!

I had never seen an Asian restaurant or ever eaten Chinese food. In addition, I had never had an adventurous palate. I had always had a very sensitive digestive system and tried new foods usually to my peril. I recognized some of the vegetables. They also had a large bowl of lettuce, tomatoes, and salad dressings. I concentrated on those foods, safely keeping up my ruse but also protecting my stomach.

I was very uncomfortable during our dinner and could not wait to get home. Asa drove back to the mortuary school parking lot where my truck sat alone. He did not ask me, he just gently kissed me as I got out of the car. I was not ready for any type of physical affection. The pain of my last relationship breakup was still too real.

For a week or two, I avoided him at all costs. I wanted him to just leave me alone. I was intent on getting my associate degree in applied science, getting a job, and getting on with my life. I was not available for any more physical, emotional, or psychological pain.

Chapter 16

Secrets Revealed

Mrs. Petty became more and more demanding and restrictive about the house rules for Brittany and me. I lost the opportunity for a good 3:00 p.m. to 11:00 p.m. night job that I desperately needed to survive financially. Because of the odd hours I was available because of school, I applied for evening jobs—nursing homes, hospitals, security companies, and mortuary services. School was very hard, but I had no choice about working.

Mrs. Petty's rules required that we both had to be inside and the doors locked at 8:00 p.m. Her demands were becoming harder and harder to abide by, but there was no way I could rent a place by myself.

Brittany was the eternal optimist type of personality who was a pro at making lemonade out of lemons. She insisted we study together in each other's rooms after the front and back doors to the residence were locked at 8:00 p.m. each night. During our times together, we became close friends.

One night after finishing our homework, Brittany said, "Tell me about your first sexual experience. My parents are both psychologists, and I love to hear friends' life stories—if you are comfortable enough to tell me."

I proceeded to tell her about my relationship with Ricky, the good and the bad. "Bastard!" she said, after hearing of the abuse at the end of our relationship. "Why can't people just enjoy each other instead of sabotaging a good thing?

"I'm so sorry that happened to you. Sounds to me like he just tricked you and took advantage of you. If you were just fifteen, and he was twenty-four, I think that was child abuse or something. He probably should have been put in jail. No telling how many other people he did that to. Makes me sick. Mmmm, funny—not funny-funny but strange—it still sounds like you are carrying a torch for him. Was he always mean to you?"

"No, he couldn't have been nicer at first, but that didn't last but a short few months before he started knocking me around," I explained. "Sorry for getting off on a tangent. My feelings about Ricky are hard to explain. He was not my first, but he was my first consensual relationship. That made him special. He just could not be faithful to me. When people told me on several occasions that they saw him at a club French kissing someone else while we were going together, I did not believe them.

"One night Nancy, Butch, and Betsy showed up at Mae and Leon's house and rushed me out the door to their car. It was a hot, muggy night, and they drove me straight to Ricky's house, where the door was standing wide open. He was still sitting in his recliner, where they had seen him only minutes before, hugging and kissing a young boy."

Brittany interrupted as she stated, disgusted, "And you saw this with your own eyes?" as she held her hand over her heart.

I proceeded to explain, "It would be an understatement to say I was devastated. I hated so much for them to be right. For months I grieved the loss of that relationship. I would go out on occasion with my girlfriends and flirt and dance, but anything more was too difficult for me, until one night they insisted I go with them to a local club just to get out of the house.

"That was the first time I had ever been to a nightclub of any kind. I was only seventeen at the time, but I was with my adult guardians, Mae and Leon, and the manager knew them all too well and let me stay without further questioning.

"There was a dancer there who at first sight made me forget all about Ricky." I laughed a nervous laugh.

Brittany excitedly interrupted, "Well, finally. It serves that pervert Ricky right ... but go ahead and finish. I'm so sorry I interrupted you."

"It's okay," I stated as I lightly laughed. "The dancer was amazing. His name was Steven. We started dancing, and I knew he was the one for me for life. The traits that attracted me to him, however, became the traits that ultimately ruined our relationship for all the wrong reasons.

"All right," Brittany shouted. "I'm just sad it ended poorly before I even know what happened."

"Sorry for the spoiler," I continued. "He was in his forties and was very kind, gentle, generous, and patient with me. He left thank you and love notes everywhere he knew I would find them. He was the first person who was more interested in satisfying me sexually than in my satisfying him. I felt guilty that I was not really attracted to him.

"I later realized in therapy that my attraction to him ended because I was unfamiliar and uncomfortable with kindness, peace, and love in a relationship. Actually, I was bored. I absolutely hated all the chaos I had grown up in, but chaos was familiar and had become my normal.

"I regretfully admit, looking back, that for once in my life I wanted and needed to be the back walking away. My selfishness in that relationship and how I hurt him haunts me to this day. I'm having a profound feeling of guilt and sadness right now just talking about it.

"After several months of relationships with several unsuitable partners, a pattern was emerging. Relationship after relationship, I was doing the cooking, the cleaning, the laundry, and the grocery shopping. I was drawing the hot bath water, putting on the soft music, and lighting the scented candles, but nothing I did was enough. My resentment started out like cold water in a pressure cooker on a hot burner.

"I realized I was doing all the giving when my resentment reached the boiling point. I went on strike. The cupboards were bare, no dinner was cooked, and there were no clean clothes. Clutter was everywhere. No hot bath was drawn, no soft music was playing, and no candles were flickering. I had not showered, shaved, or washed my hair.

"When my partner at the time named Bert came home that night, the pressure cooker blew (for both of us), and World War III broke out. He slapped me into a wall for being lazy. He stormed out of the house, leaving, he said, 'for good.' While crying face down on the bed like my mom used to do, writhing in pain with a cup towel stuffed up my nose to stop the bleeding, I wrote this poem:

"Givers search for takers to make them feel complete.
Takers chase the givers, and sweep them off their feet.
Together they are one,
And happiness will reign
Until the giver's done, and no takers remain."

"Wow, James. How good you got counseling. How did you afford it?"

I answered, "That therapy was ordered by the court after I ended up at the hospital with an unsuccessful suicide attempt while I was in high school. I resented having to go, but it was one of the best things I've ever done."

"You probably can predict my next question," she said.

"No, what it is?" I responded, puzzled.

"You said Ricky was not your first but your first consensual relationship. Want to tell me about your first? It's okay if it's too painful. Sometimes it loses its power if you let it out. That's what

I've heard both my parents say over and over. They say we are as sick as our secrets, and I want to assure you that your secret will be safe with me."

My first reaction to Brittany's question was that she had gone too far. Telling her about my sexual history was painful but okay. Telling her about Uncle Bruce would be a different matter entirely, but she was persuasive, and I decided to take a risk.

"You will be the first person I have ever told about this incident. I knew my girlfriends back home would run their heads and get both my uncle and me in trouble, so I've had no one to tell. My mandated therapist in high school almost got me to tell, but I knew she would be making life-and-death decisions about school, so I chose to clam up right before it came out to her."

"Oh, no, hurry and tell me. It must have been something bad," she said compassionately.

For the next few minutes I told her about my encounters with Uncle Bruce. Brittany was more than pleased when I told her he was dead. *Maybe Brittany should be a therapist like her parents,* I remembered thinking to myself. After telling her part of my story, I felt a great sense of relief. Until it all came out, I never knew the agony I had been in, holding it all inside.

"You said you had three younger brothers. How did they and their friends handle your being gay?"

"You'll probably be interested in a regression I had during therapy. That will explain it, I think. The bullies in school were the older brothers of my classmates. When my classmates gradually got older and started mimicking their older brothers' rants, those times, I must admit, were terribly painful. I remember like it was yesterday the day that my inward pain reached an almost unbearable level—a level so great that I learned I had repressed the memory of the incident for years.

"My brother Adam, nearest in age to me, was called by Harry's drinking buddies 'the perfect man's man.' He was born knowing how to pitch and hit a baseball, throw and catch a football, and run like the wind. Harry would brag that Adam was the way a perfect boy should be and was, without a doubt, his biological son. It was obvious to all the backyard beer-drinking clan that someone else had to have fathered Adam's sissy older brother.

"Many years later, when Adam became an award-winning, bull-riding rodeo star, my dad's life, in his words, was proven worthwhile. We were all grown at the time, but my dad bought him an expensive pair of leather chaps to protect him since he was so important to him.

"He told Adam in front of my other brothers and me that he would die if anything happened to his favorite son. That was the only gift to any of his sons I ever remember my dad buying.

"Some of the most back-slapping laughter at the beer-drinking backyard parties was guessing which pervert/fag in town had fathered me. The first time I overheard those bastards laughing about my being a bastard, I have to admit I wanted to die. That pain was almost unbearable.

"Oddly enough, however, I eventually became immune to their fun at my expense because secretly I came to believe that they were right. I came to believe that my real father was not the town reprobate. In my opinion, the town's reprobate was really the bastard now married to my mother, and according to his own words, he was thankfully no kin to me.

"There was a short window of time when Adam and I were the same size, just before he shot up a lot taller than I. At that time, people would often ask if we were twins. It never occurred to me how to explain the fact that Adam and I looked so much alike and had different fathers. That would have been getting into a genetic realm that was way above my frame of reference or interest in junior high.

"When my time to speak in the group arrived, the therapist asked me to tell her about my family. Without any emotion, I gave her a brief clinical description of my parents and brothers. She was already aware of my relationship with both of my parents. She had requested information about my relationship with my brothers on several occasions, but I would emphatically tell her there was nothing to tell her that I hadn't already told her.

"On this occasion, however, she instinctively went right to the heart of the matter, refusing to accept no for an answer. She requested and insisted I tell her in more detail about my brothers.

"I tearfully told her and the group that I felt more like their father than a brother. I had loved and protected them by staying up every night until my parents and they were all asleep to make sure my dad wasn't beating them.

"On many occasions I would sneak a clean, empty bowl and can opener out of the kitchen, put it under my pillow, and sneak down to my aunt Rosie's house (knowing her back door by the kitchen would be unlocked) to steal fruit, a slice of bread, and a cookie or two for each of us, or a can or two of vegetables from her pantry.

"My brother Adam's favorite stolen supper was a slice of amazingly soft (not week old like we were used to) Wonder Bread dipped in a can of cold pork and beans, mixed with a can of cold stewed tomatoes in the carefully hidden bowl. Only rich people had microwaves, so getting out and washing pots and pans would make too much noise and wake one or both of my parents.

"My brother Joseph's favorite meal was soft white Wonder Bread smeared with Kraft Miracle Whip and cold sliced Spam. We never had those items at our house. Once when I opened a pilfered can of SPAM, liquid spilled everywhere, and my dad beat us all because he said our room smelled like "a whorehouse." He demanded to know if we had had girls sneak into our bedroom. We had no idea what in the world he was talking about.

"With my brothers' bellies full, I would sneak to the kitchen, put the can opener back in the drawer, wash the telltale signs off the soiled bowl and spoons, dry them off, and put them quietly back exactly where I had gotten them. I would quickly finish this task, and my brothers would be sleeping soundly after gorging by the time I got back to the bedroom.

"On many other occasions," I continued sharing in my group, "I would remind my dad that I was his sissy son and the one he was really mad at, instead of the brother or mom he was raging at prior to starting a beating. At age thirteen, I bought my two younger brothers at the time their first pair of store-bought jeans with some of the first money I made at the funeral home.

"When Adam wanted to play football his first year of junior high, I borrowed money against my next paycheck from Mr. Pastore to buy him the list of everything that he had to furnish to be able to play. I left work early to attend Adam's first football game.

"I was a born cheerleader type and loudly cheered him on because I was so proud of him. He was really, really good at football. My dad had asked me so many times why I couldn't be more like Adam. That afternoon I asked myself that same sad, rhetorical, unanswerable question.

"After finishing this sentence in the group, I began to sob uncontrollably, lowered my head, and covered my eyes with my hands, remembering back and trying to hide the shame. I remember saying, 'You can't make me tell you any more.'

"The therapist skillfully asked a question that brought me gently from my gut back to my head, and then she unobtrusively and painstakingly escorted me back to the edge of the psychological black hole I felt I was being inexorably sucked into.

"Assured I was in a safe place among friends (not to mention the fact that my grade point average was in the balance), I surrendered trustingly but was sobbing so hard no one could understand me. I grabbed my knees with my hands, swung my feet up onto the couch to my left, and went into a fetal position, my head glued to the top of my knocking knees, soaking my jeans with my tears.

"Looking back, I'm sure my therapist was both surprised and relieved when I finally got the story out. My pain was in my reliving that experience, based on our long and painful history as brothers. I was convinced that our lifelong jointly experienced pain and suffering, both personally and as a witness of the abuse of someone we loved, had bonded us for life. No one could fully understand that invisible, albeit imaginary bond, unless they had experienced it.

"After that first game of football, Adam had made a game-winning play in a lip- biting, jaw-dropping end to a game. As it ended, I raced onto the field, grabbed him from behind, and hugged him with all my might. He pulled away and acted like he didn't even know me.

"I had been home long enough to help Mom by hanging wet clothes on the fence, rehearsing in my head how I would tell him how proud I was of his spectacular and thrilling performance. I looked up just in time to see Adam lunging at me, as mad as I had ever seen him. I instinctively stepped out of the way as he raced full speed ahead into the dilapidated fence, riding it to the ground and bloodying his nose.

"I ran into the house to get a cold wet rag to clean his nose, and he screamed loudly, 'Do not ever come to one of my games again! Do not ever even act like you know me in public. Never, ever touch me in front of any of my friends again!'

"He raised his voice to its highest decibel and screamed, 'And while I'm at it, stop, stop, stop walking and talking like a girl! You make me sick! Just forget you ever knew me,' he said as he lowered his cracking, hormonal voice and ran into the house, bleeding and sobbing.

"Sticks and stones may break my bones, but words will never harm me." Really?

Mrs. Petty banged on my door about that time, opened the door furiously, and said she had had all the noise she could stand. She raged about how she had to get up early the next morning and accused us of being several negative adjectives.

Now, not only could we not leave the house after 8:00 p.m.,

but we also had to be quiet as well. The next day I called my Aunt Rene and told her I would be moving in with her and traveling back and forth each day. She told me I could earn part of my rent by keeping her house spotless for her. That would be a win/win, we both agreed.

Asa helped me move in with them, and Aunt Rene fell in love with him. I told her I was not interested in a relationship with the hard schoolwork I was tackling, but she saw things differently and just could not accept what I was telling her.

My Uncle Carlos was a man of many talents with a fantastic sense of humor. He affectionately called me either Gertrude or Trudie, and he was very persuasive. He was a used car salesman and could talk anybody into anything.

Aunt Rene turned out to be the angry, deceitful, and controlling gossip other family members had accused her of being. I really didn't know her that well prior to moving in with her. She jumps to conclusions and excommunicates any family member who questions or crosses her. She is known for not speaking to any given part of the family for years at a time. I've often wondered what happened to her brother, Harry, and her to make them the way they turned out.

One Friday on the phone to my aunt, letting her know I was leaving school to come back for the weekend, she said, "We are all going to dress up and go to a nice dinner tonight." I was not thrilled since the drive and schoolwork were beginning to stress me out, but wanting to keep the peace, faking cheerfulness, I agreed.

Strangely, but unfortunately characteristically, she insisted I change my outfit three times before she agreed I had put on the perfect one. As we were about to leave for the car, the doorbell rang. She quickly said, "Please don't be mad at me. That's Asa. He's a really nice guy, James, and he really likes you. We've invited him to go to dinner with us."

What? How could they have done this to me? I was furious

but maintained my cool, and we went out and had a nice dinner. I even enjoyed myself. Exhausted, though, I insisted Asa get back on the road so he would not have to be out too late. My aunt insisted he spend the night since the next day was a weekend. I was being ganged up on, I thought.

My aunt had never cooked breakfast in the past to my knowledge, but the next morning she got up early and put out her finest dishes and silverware around the table. We had always helped ourselves to the pots on the stove and taken our plate to the TV room on the rare occasions I had eaten at her house in the past.

She cooked crisp bacon, eggs cooked to order, and pancakes for all of us. When Asa left after breakfast, I got into an argument with my aunt. She was furious with me, and I was furious with her. I did not tell her that I had made the decision to see Asa again, but I felt strongly that was my decision, not hers.

Even though I resented the way I felt everyone was trying to manipulate and/or control my life, there was something really special about Asa that I was having difficulty pinpointing.

As bad as I tried not to, I could not stop thinking about him and his kindness. He was not the type of man I was usually attracted to, and I did not understand my growing interest in him. Maybe I was getting another chance for a relationship with a really nice guy, I hoped deep down. Maybe this one would turn out better than the last one.

Most of the men I had previously dated were alpha type males, much more like Harry, as much as I hated him. Those relationships had inevitably ended in predictably (to everyone but me) disastrous ways. My attempts to mend my relationship with Harry through relationships with the same type of angry, often abusive alcoholic choices, had not worked out well at all.

"Maybe I should give Asa another chance," I had written one night in the journal on my nightstand beside the bed. I was surprised the next morning when I read the entry, because I had no memory of writing it the night before.

CHAPTER 17

MY ASA

Asa and I went to eat another couple of times in Dallas. On one occasion he had left his wallet at home and said we were going by so he could pick it up. He insisted that I come in with him so he could show me his place. I was blown away. He had his very own, brand new apartment.

I sat down on a beautiful dark leather sectional that was a hide-a-bed in the large middle section. I had never seen one of those! The two pieces on each end were recliners with consoles in the middle.

Asa had several unpacked boxes in the corner, with one huge picture of Marilyn Monroe standing against the wall. All he had done when moving in was hang up his clothes and empty an overnight bag with toiletries. All the appliances had a new shiny black porcelain finish with beautiful gray-black-and-white countertops.

The bathroom had a hotel-type mirror that wrapped around where you could see the back of your head! There was clutter everywhere. Every surface had open school-books and notebooks.

I started visualizing pictures on the wall and sheers on the windows in brighter colors to lighten and cheer the place up. More than I wanted to go to dinner—and I was very hungry—I secretly wished we could just order pizza and stay there. I could help him get the boxes empty and put away. Fortunately for him, he would soon learn I hated clutter more than he didn't mind it.

My imagination was running wild. I caught myself thinking that this place needed me. I had been complaining at school about Aunt Rene's controlling and meddling. He suggested I move in with him, just as a friend. I could not only save my money, he continued, but I could also get away from my aunt.

While he went to the bedroom to get his wallet, I sat on the middle section of the sectional, and it literally engulfed and caressed me. I looked at the new glass-top table, and my heart went to my toes in shock and fear. There was a rolled-up dollar bill and white residue of powder on the table. What had I done? Was I dating a druggy?

He walked back in, saw what I was looking at, and said, "I have friends who do drugs. They left those items there last night." I told him I had done drugs but was off of them for good.

We never made it to dinner. I woke up the next morning in bed with him as the alarm went off. I was horrified. I had to get away from him. My life and my education were on the line. I told him to lose my number and never call me again.

I repeatedly turned down Asa's suggestions of things we could do together. I finally told him to leave me alone and to never call me again. He then started avoiding and ignoring me at school. While I was relieved, I had some of the all-too-familiar feelings of sadness, loss, and even abandonment. I was convinced I was crazy.

I got a call from Betsy at an especially low time. After filling her in on all the details, she said, "James, everything I hear about Asa makes me like him more, not the other way around. He sounds like a really nice guy to me. True, he's not the type you usually pick, but maybe you finally deserve a nice guy.

"Why don't you just date him for a few times? At least he's not the kind of jerk, stuck on himself, that you usually go for. And don't act like you don't know what I'm talking about." Her words fell on deaf ears. Asa had stopped calling, and there was no way my pride would allow me to call him.

Semester finals were nearing, and I buried myself in the books. School was very difficult! I had been out of school so long that the cobwebs were deeply entrenched. Not only that, I'm sure I had lost many brain cells from drinking and drugging. On more than one occasion I was sure I had made a wrong decision about even coming to school.

Relations between my aunt and me were icy, to say the least. I had had the audacity to cross her. She was obviously looking for some excuse to punish me for rejecting her attempts at matchmaking. When an argument started over a really insignificant matter, she came undone.

She had all my clothes packed up and sitting at the door the next morning. She told me how disappointed she was in me and how wrong she had been about me. No wonder my dad had kicked me out, she shouted as I picked up my suitcases and headed for my pickup.

I loaded my pickup and headed out of town. I had errands I needed to do in a nearby larger town. I got to a major intersection that turned out to be a major turning point in my life. I considered turning left and heading back home, admitting defeat, or turning right and heading back to Dallas, completing my education.

If I turned left and headed back to Tumbleweed, I would have several places I would be welcome to spend the night, no questions asked. Turning right, I would have to start sleeping in my car again.

As I sat there, time stood still. As I equivocated, I began to shake all over with tears pouring down my cheeks. In a moment of sudden clarity, I knew that there was no way I could turn back and lose all I had dreamed about for many years. It would not be easy, but the turn to the right won out. I was energized and motivated. I was excited, knowing I'd made the right decision.

As I approached the city limits of Dallas with my pickup full of all my things, I decided to make another turn that led to Asa's apartment. My rationale: I thought it would be safer to sleep in front of his house than in the neighborhood near the mortuary school. Also, I could not risk being discovered sleeping in my car after I had begged the registrar to let me stay, assuring her I could afford to stay in school.

I pulled in front of his house, where he was standing around with a bunch of friends from school. As soon as they saw me, they made excuses and disappeared. I told him I had been thrown out of my aunt's house and just wanted to sleep in my truck in a safer neighborhood. He led me on a while, being cool and distant because he had been deeply hurt by my behavior, and then he shyly invited me in.

"Look. First I want to apologize for the way I've been treating you. I want you to understand that that's about me and has nothing to do with you. You seem to be a great guy with a lot of potential. You are just the kind of person so many people are looking for in a relationship.

"You are kind, smart, competent, and even-tempered. Nothing seems to upset you. You are so many of the things I have wanted to be but knew I could never be."

"Does your moving in as a friend have to be complicated? I'd just like you to have a place to stay, and I could use the company. I promise not to put more on you than you are ready or willing to do. Whether or not the relationship ever goes any further than that is fine with me."

We talked all night about our expectations for a relationship. We opened up and told each other a lot of our history of being gay in a hostile small town. So much of our histories were things we had in common.

Things were going well until we hit a snag. I told him that the next relationship I got in would have to give me one thing that was more important to me than anything in the whole world. For a few minutes, it looked like the immovable object had just met the irresistible force. I asked him to please hear me out.

"From an early age," I started out, "my deepest desire was to be a dad. I have wanted children more than anything in the world for as long as I can remember. I want children to love like I was never loved but always longed to be. I want children I can support in being the best they can be with whatever gifts or orientation they were naturally born with.

"I love to clean house, cook, and nurture the wounded in my social sphere. A lot of my time for most of my life has been devoted to helping female friends and coworkers who were in abusive relationships, especially those with young children.

"When sober, I have experienced moments of profound sadness that two men cannot reproduce. Is my dream of being a father something I will never know, I have often wondered?

"Based on my history that I've told you about tonight, I'm seriously afraid that even a fulfilling, loving relationship with a man seems way too far out of my reach. No matter how great a relationship for me has started out, every time, without exception, the dream has turned into a nightmare. The only conclusion I've been able to reach is that I am the problem. I'm a mistake, fatally flawed, just like Harry always told me. You deserve better than me, Asa, truly.

"Do you have any thoughts about what I've told you so far?"

Asa responded with a sad look on his face. "For all the reasons you have given me tonight about why you want to be a dad—all those same reasons are why I've never wanted to be a dad.

"How would I be able to be the kind of father I would need to be if I am fatally flawed, as you put it? Kids might love me when they were little, but when they got a little older and their friends started making fun of their dad, or two dads, as you and I know they would, how would that work out? I would never want to intentionally put that burden on a child that did not ask to be born."

I said, "When I was in high school, the best catch in the school asked me to go to the prom when she broke up with her boyfriend. She just wanted to wear her new dress and say she had been to her high school prom. We had a great time because we were just friends, but all the bullies who had given me grief since I started school all of a sudden got nicer.

"Reports came back to me that they could not believe how wrong they had been about me. When my friend Betsy hung around me at school, we plotted for her to show me affection, and for a short time no one bullied me. When they thought I was *normal,* I was a regular guy, but that only lasted a short time until they figured out she was in love with my brother.

"When the bullies thought I was gay, my life was constantly in the balance. I truly did not know from one day to the next if I would live another day.

"Because of the relief after the prom, I seriously considered finding a compatible woman, settling down, and marrying her. This way, I could prove that all the bullies who had called me vile names from the second grade on, including my dad, were all wrong.

"I had not at the time, nor have I ever had, the slightest desire for a sexual encounter with a woman. That was the reason I was devastated when the first guy I dated accused me of having an affair with Betsy. He was so wrong, and that was so painful to me.

"This was a serious problem that tortured me for over a year. Any woman I would care enough about to marry to be the mother of my children, I would care too much about to subject her to the pain and rejection of a husband not attracted to her. Also, proving an untruth at a dear friend's expense was something I could not bring myself to do.

"I had a wonderful, close female friend, Heather, who was attracted to women, and we both wanted children. We decided to have sex so she could carry a baby for us to co-parent. The time came for the clinical activity, but neither of us could follow through on our plan.

"We both cried about what we were considering doing. We analyzed our motives during an emotional four-hour encounter and conversation and decided that we cared too much about one another to just use one another for our own selfish ends.

"Also, we concluded that would not be a positive way to bring a child into the world. What if we later broke up or could not agree over the parenting of the child? There were just too many possibilities for disaster for us to follow through with it, and I'm really glad we didn't. We are still dear friends to this day, though.

"Okay, how about this? If we live together for a while and things are working out, would you consider fostering some children who have been in the same situation we've been in? Could we just consider being there for kids who are being abused and are confused? You don't have to agree to it right now, but please just think about it. I want you to remember, though, how important it is for me to be a parent one day. That is truly not negotiable."

We have been together ever since. Maybe there was, I thought, the Big God after all. What had been my slowly evolving faith of disbelief was being seriously questioned.

When Asa would be too kind or nice to me, upsetting me because of the unfamiliarity with his kind behavior, I thought back to the many mistakes I had made, not thinking I deserved that kind of treatment. I was determined to learn from those past regretted mistakes.

We both had good jobs very soon and were doing better financially. Classes lasted until 12:30 p.m. each day and then dismissed for everyone to go to their jobs. We both worked from 3:00 p.m. to 11:00 p.m. at sister nursing homes, caring for the elderly and doing any odd jobs that needed to be done.

Every day I was grateful we both had jobs. There was no way I could have survived without being given a job on many occasions.

Looking back, I'm not sure I can explain how we did it all— going to school, caring for kids, working at a job, making financial ends meet, fostering crack-addicted newborns and at-risk children, and caring for an elderly person in our home.

Our lives were a constant deadline that had to be reached or we could lose everything. The only explanation I have is that we just did it one day at a time. Actually, many times a day was too much to tackle at a time. During those times we just lived from moment to moment, but somehow we survived.

Asa gets so much credit for his levelheaded calmness that counterbalanced my off-the-wall ADHD and desire for constant perfection in all areas of life. Because of our differences, we clashed a lot, but we have also gained a lot of love and forgiveness for each other's shortcomings during our years together.

When I was given the job of cleaning the restrooms at the nursing home—a job, I was secretly told by a nurse, that was always given to the new employees as a test of their work ethic, attitude, thoroughness, and ability to handle unpleasant tasks—I asked my supervisor if he thought he could get me some white vinegar and bleach so I could clean the restroom like Aunt Luann had taught me when visiting her in the summers. My supervisor elatedly called me aside in a few days and told me the bathrooms had never been cleaner and the entire home had never smelled better.

During summer vacations at Aunt Luann's house, the same bottles would still be there from the summer before. Aunt Luann never used them herself, but she taught me what her grandmother had taught her. The first thing I did each summer at her house was to find the bottles of vinegar and bleach and clean the restrooms so my brothers and I would not get a bad disease.

After Asa and I had been together several months, there was a knock on the door. Standing on the inside of that knocking door, I was a single young man with his whole life in front of him, obsessed with the single-minded pursuit of an education.

The highest joy—and knowledge of the lowest betrayal of my life—stood on the other side of that door. I opened the door, perturbed I was being interrupted from my studies, and there stood an older woman with a baby girl in her arms, with an older girl holding her hand beside her.

She bluntly asked, "Who are you?"

I answered curtly, "I think the question is who are you, and what are you doing here?" It soon become clear I had not started out on a good foot with Asa's mother.

She answered curtly that she was Asa's mother, and these were Asa's children. "Where is Asa?" she demanded to know.

We had been living a lie. Asa had been married and divorced and had two children! Asa's mother had brought them for the first court-ordered visit of one week a month. My life changed irreversibly in that moment.

We had no time to fight over the irreversible, game-changing decision he had made to withhold this important information from me. The two-month-old baby, Leah, had to be fed and changed. The four-year-old, Ashira, was hungry, too. Asa and I sprang into action, alternately angry and snarky with each other under our breath.

I soon invested my heart and soul into these two precious, innocent lives, neither of whom had asked to be born. I smiled when I learned that both girls coincidentally had Jewish names. As hard as I tried not to at first, I fell in love with the two-month-old first, then with the four-year-old.

At first, the four-year-old was skeptical of me and what I was up to. I had to earn her confidence and love, but it didn't take long. The first thing I did was cut Ashira's hair. Her bangs and locks were all crooked, and her hair was like straw. She loved the transformation! I had always loved fixing hair and applying makeup and nail polish. As soon as I got her all fixed up, she was an instant friend and admirer.

These little people were astonishingly smart. They both loved to be read to. I had always been a neatnic, cleaning, straightening up, and probably symbolically trying to bring order out of the chaos I had been born into, before I could do anything else.

Before the children joined us, Asa would often beg me to come watch a TV show with him right after dinner, but I could not sit down nor rest until all clutter was cleared from every room, the dishes were clean and put away, the floors swept and mopped, one load of laundry was in the dryer and another was washing, and the bathrooms were spotless.

I would often smile to myself when my obsession with cleaning and straightening up first, before doing anything else, moved to second place. I caught myself plopping down in the middle of scattered toys, dishes left in the sink after dinner, dirty clothes and wet towels on the floor of the bathroom as I read a book, sang to, and put my freshly fed and bathed babies to sleep.

Those previously urgent chores started waiting for me until the more important matters were attended to. More important than anything in the world to me became that my kids were sleeping safely in their beds, knowing they were loved and away from harm each night.

Of all the pain I had experienced in my life, none compared to the moment when Asa's mother would drive away with the kids until the next month's visitation. This went on for years until we got full custody of them. Her driving out of the driveway would usually come after Leah would literally have to be peeled away from me, and Ashira would be crying in Asa's arms, screaming angrily, "Why do we always have to leave?"

Every time they left, my heart would be beating excessively with an indescribable ache in my chest. Tears would be streaming down my face, and the loss would soon overtake me. Almost every time they left, I would go inside, take an Excedrin PM, and sleep for the next twelve hours to escape the emotional pain.

One Saturday around 3:00 p.m., I had a deadline due on a paper for my online class, so I went inside, starting clearing up the toys and clutter from the kids, and putting everything in the house back in order, dreading getting back on the computer. I had been mentally blocked for some time on this paper and didn't know why.

There was a knock on the door. As I opened the door, a young lady said, "Hi, I'm Gretchen. I'm Asa's friend from his old apartments.

Gretchen had lived in the same apartment complex with Asa his first year at school. Her hair was cut in a short spike, and it was colored purple to match her outfit. She wore a gorgeous purple and fuchsia American Indian necklace she had bought back home in Sedona, Arizona, a fuchsia outfit, fuchsia eye shadow, and purple shoes. Gretchen was anything but forgettable. From that day forward, she became Quirky Gretchen to me.

In all the commotion of getting the kids ready to leave, Asa had not had the chance to tell me an old friend Gretchen had called, and he had offered our house for a surprise birthday party for one of the old friends from his old apartment complex—that night!

I was furious with Asa. *How could he do this to me?* I fumed to myself. *He knows I have a deadline, the house is a wreck from the kids, and now we have to get the place ready for a birthday party?* Gretchen and two other friends had arrived to start the decorating. What was I going to do?

While Gretchen motioned to her two friends in the car to start unloading her car, Asa took me aside and said, "Look. Please calm down. You won't have to do anything. We'll do all the cleaning up, the furniture rearranging, putting up the chairs, etc. Here, I'll put this TV table and folding chair in the bedroom closet, and you can close the door and finish your paper. No harm, no foul."

As I closed the bedroom door and sat down, my blood pressure lowered, and I felt a sense of calm I had not felt for weeks. I realized I was once again at home, secluded in a cozy closet!

My energy soared. The words flew off the end of my fingers onto the computer screen. My mind was clear, my body was comfortable, and my recall was better than it had been in weeks. I hit the send button on a paper I was very proud of at 10:53 p.m., over an hour ahead of time!

As I emerged from the bedroom, the living room was completely rearranged, the place was spotless, and all the decorations were up and ready. All of the guests had been there an hour or two and were helping themselves to snacks and drinks.

Gretchen, I learned, was a feng shui expert. After I emerged, she looked into the bedroom and said, "It's a wonder you ever get a good night's rest the way your bed is facing." Before she left, she instructed us on how to turn our bed around to face the opposite direction, and I absolutely loved all the changes. I gave her all the credit for my renewed mental acuity, physical vigor, and improving grades.

Before that day I had known nothing about New Age, vortices, crystals, or feng shui. But just to be safe, for years after that, every new place we moved into was preceded by a call to Gretchen, making sure that the closet we picked for my desk and computer were correctly positioned.

While I went home for the holidays during my second year in school, Gretchen took pictures she had taken of our new apartment, and she and a friend spent untold hours figuring out suggestions on how to rearrange the furniture, which direction for me to face in which closet while I was studying, and which direction to face the bed, and she said, "Now I feel so much better. Your schoolwork will be at least ten times easier." She was right, and I gave her all the credit.

CHAPTER 18

JEWISH ROOTS

D uring the second year at mortuary school, I landed a highly coveted job at a prestigious funeral home that specialized in conducting Jewish funerals. Every student at mortuary school wanted an internship or job at this funeral home for his/her résumé.

The curriculum at the school I attended did not offer the course that eventually would make such a profound difference in my life. Only this type of change could have been orchestrated by a higher power.

The owner of the funeral home, Marilyn Holmes, took me under her wing and was very kind, accepting, and loving toward me. Her appearance personified understated elegance. Her clothing screamed "expensive" to a kid from a small town. I was in awe of her good looks, her immaculate dress, her flawless grooming, and her business acumen.

Marilyn lived in a beautiful apartment upstairs in the funeral home. She laughingly joked one day about how much she hated to clean and organize her bedroom closet and how very badly it needed it. I excitedly told her I was very good at organizing things and anytime she wanted to give me a chance to help her, I would be thrilled.

Our next slow day, she took me up to her closet to work.

Since childhood, I had loved the intimacy and safeness of a closet. I absolutely fell in love with this part of my job. Fantasizing alone in her fabulous closet that was bigger than my bedroom growing up was a dream come true! In addition, I got a crash course in all the famous designer perfumes, bags, shoes, scarves, jewelry, and dresses.

She also gave me a crash course in Jewish history, the Hebrew language, and the ancient Jewish funeral customs. I was fascinated; I could not get enough. She gave me a book to learn the Jewish prayers that would be used during the burials.

There is usually no embalming of the body in Jewish tradition. The men carefully bathe and clothe the males in a tachrichim, a hand-sewn white linen shroud, and the women bathe and clothe the females in the same fashion.

A shomer (body watcher) is with the body at all times until Kevurah (the burial). Chevra Kadisha, the Hebrew burial society, takes care of all the rituals associated with the burial. The first hesped (eulogy) I heard delivered by Rabbi Weinstein had a profound effect on me.

My square corners were gradually, albeit with deep anguish and pain, being rounded off my square edges. And in another big bang moment, I would soon fit perfectly into the round hole waiting for me since birth—handed down from my mother, who was born Jewish.

I grew close to one of the regular shomers from a local synagogue named Chloe. She was also very kind to me, answering all my nonstop questions about Judaism. On more than one occasion I stayed late with her, discussing burning concerns I had never had anyone I could ask.

One morning, as dawn arrived, we both laughed when we realized I had never gone home and I was also almost late for class at school! The weight of the world was lifted from my shoulders when she explained to me the Jewish theology about heaven and hell.

Jewish theology does not subscribe to the concept of hell. For years I had had nightmares about the flames coming up and the Big God dropping me in the hole because of my bad deeds and because of Harry's imprecations that God should judge me harshly. I learned that night that hell is a Christian concept.

In Judaism, observance of Yom Kippur is the annual spiritual washing of a person's sins on earth. The shomer washes the body of a deceased person, and the soul goes to a place where it is washed and cleansed before it is rejoined with God in heaven. Every aspect of Judaism both thrilled and enthralled me. I had finally arrived at home spiritually.

I felt God's forgiveness and permission for the first time for being the person I was born to be and for redeeming all the bad deeds of my life. I had come home after wandering without a compass in my own, mostly self-imposed desert. I looked up and thanked God for the manna he had sent that had sustained me through all my suffering and disbelief.

I thanked Him for never turning his back on me in my desert but always facing me with open arms and, like adjusting the lens on a telescope, miraculously bringing into sharp focus the lights of the Promised Land.

A different type of suffering and rejection, however, was just beginning. My conversion brought another type of condemnation. I had just added another reason for vile slurs, misunderstanding, and abandonment from, predictably, the same uninformed, often irreligious acquaintances and family members.

That kind of person will always exist. With the help of a loving rabbi, I now know whom to blame. She helped me see that I had been blaming the Big God for everything bad that was happening to me instead of the perpetrators in my life. She also taught me that the forgiveness I will continually be working on for every person who has harmed me since childhood is really for me and not for them.

I became active in a synagogue after that rich work experience and have been so blessed to bring my children up in the Jewish faith and with a Jewish education. Both our oldest girls had a b'not mitzvah in June of 2015, and the youngest daughter, Adiyah, nine years old, is already studying to be a future rabbi.

If you hate me because I'm a Jew,
There is nothing I can do.
That title was given to me
By a woman I never knew.

My growing exposure to different aspects of the art and science of the funeral business delighted and intrigued me, but something was still missing. The left side of my brain was being engaged, but I also felt more and more the need to engage more of the right brain in my business life.

Since I was so small and young (and always looked even younger than I was), especially when I started, I mostly stayed silent when attending to the needs of the bereaved at viewings. What does a kid know about death and dying anyway?

In my silence, however, I was carefully observing and absorbing the psychology of death and grieving and the many different ways people go through the process. My education was constantly evolving and was not only from textbooks.

More and more I was helping the bereaved handle their grief, but I realized I needed a bachelor's degree to be able to use it in any meaningful way. While working for the Jewish funeral home, this fact was becoming clearer and clearer to me as I signed up for online classes to continue my education.

CHAPTER 19

THROWAWAY KID

After graduating from mortuary school with an associate's degree in funeral service, we moved to a town near my Aunt Rene where we both had jobs at different funeral homes. Aunt Rene had worked for a nursing home where a resident, Louise, lived.

Louise was so belligerent and hateful to everyone in the nursing home, from the staff to the residents, that she was about to be evicted. Aunt Rene took her into her home and, past records have revealed, decided to take control of her assets and to get her monthly income.

She did just that, but after liquidating her assets of several thousand dollars a sister had left Louise, Aunt Rene decided her small Social Security check was not enough to endure Louise's hatefulness and lack of gratitude.

She called me and asked if Asa and I could keep Louise for the weekend to give her and her husband a respite. We had kept her before on short occasions without any trouble, and we agreed. Aunt Rene never came back to get her, saying she just couldn't handle her anymore.

How blessed our family was that she became Gramma Weezie to all our family and foster children. We could never countenance her going to the type of facility that would take her in for her small Social Security check.

During the twelve years she lived with us, we fostered several drug-addicted children. Most of those children screamed nonstop day and night. Not one of us could comfort most of them like Gramma Weezie could. She had large breasts and would bounce each child at night to give us a night's sleep and then nap off and on during the day. Gramma Weezie was never an interloper, although at times she was difficult to handle.

She was developmentally challenged, with anger management problems that had resulted from a childhood of some of the worst trauma imaginable. She had been locked in a basement as a child, where her brother repeatedly molested her from the age of six, followed by an uncle and then a stepdad.

When she finally opened up to us after moving in with us, and after we had read her case history, she never stopped talking about her childhood. The more she opened up and talked, the kinder and gentler she became—except for occasional episodes of flashbacks that put her into deep depression at times.

Not once in all the years before her death at home September 9, 2015, while assisted by hospice, did she ever lash out at one of the children. I am convinced that the love for and from the children is what gave her the best years of her life.

Each time Child Protective Services (CPS) would remove a child from our care when the parents got their lives back on track, our entire family would always cry. Gramma Weezie, on the other hand, would grieve for days and more than once for months. Each child became hers, and every child thought she was his/her mother.

Gramma Weezie loved to hear the stories of my childhood in and out of my childhood voice and grammar. As she got worse and worse in hospice, she would say, "Jamesy, tell me the story about the saxophone you borrowed. Now, don't never say you stole it, 'cause you didn't steal nothing. Remember, you took it back."

Watching her waste away was one of the hardest things our family ever witnessed. Recounting those childhood memories, however painful, helped take both our minds off the pain she was in near the end of her life.

At her insistence, I would tell her the story about the saxophone she insisted I borrowed in the sixth grade by starting off something like this: "During the year of the sixth grade, the abuse and volume of insults increased exponentially, and I wanted to fit in somehow so badly. Participating in sports was the typical way to achieve popularity, but I was more than athletically challenged. So, along with an older cousin and my brother Adam, we decided to get together to take a saxophone from the school band room for me to learn and master the art of being a saxophonist.

"In my mind, I imagined placing this beautiful instrument to my lips and making sounds so beautiful that everyone would stop and say, 'Wow! We've been wrong about this kid. He's a genius, he's cool, and he's the best of the best.' The plan was to borrow it, use it, learn it, and master the art, and then we would take it back and no one would even know it had been missing. In our childlike innocence, my brother, my cousin, and I figured a weekend was more than enough for me to master the saxophone.

"For weeks I struggled internally with the idea and decided no, this was not the right thing to do. I knew the commandment, 'Thou shalt not steal.' My older cousin Blake, spurred on by Jamal, insisted we do it in spite of the commandment, 'cause he told us it was owed to us anyways cause we was so poor.

"We had an argument. I told them, 'This don't feel right, and what if there really is a god and a devil? God's going to be upset, and the devil will prance around as victor.' For an instant I thought back to the picture outside the Sunday school room, and I could see myself falling into the crackling flames below.

"As I seriously wavered, Blake stated, 'Fuck it, Li'l bro, I'll do it my own damn self. You just watch. You deserve this, and I'm gonna make it happen.' School had been released early for a pep rally out on the football field in preparation for the big game that was coming up that night.

"Blake walked confidently into the emptied band room while my brother and I stood at the door, frightened and shaking. Blake casually walked out, saxophone in hand like it was his, and said, 'Okay, bro, let's make it happen. You have all weekend to study, and then we'll have it back before anyone notices that it's gone.'

"We went to Blake's house and studied and studied. The music and sounds coming from the instrument were horrid. It was nothing like Lisa Simpson played, nothing like Stevie Wonder or anyone else I'd ever heard play before.

"Every ugly thing anyone had ever thought or said about me was true. I was just a stupid fag who would never amount to anything. Failed saxophonist could now be added to my long list of failures."

I knew Weezie was nearing the end of her life when she didn't say, "No, Jamesy. You are the way you are supposed to be. Stop calling yourself a failure. You ain't no such a thing."

I would pause for her interruption, and when there was none near the end of her life—I would sadly continue, knowing she would not be with us for long. "On Sunday night, aware that we were not getting this mastered as fast as we thought we would, Blake insisted that we keep the saxophone a little longer. He was sure I would get better if I just practiced a little longer.

"The Monday after the disappointing weekend came, and the principal announced over the intercom that the instrument had been *stolen* … I was in shock. *Stolen? No!* We had just borrowed it to make my dream come true. *Oh, this is ridiculous*, I thought, *we did not steal it!* Human beings' ability to justify bad behavior did not start on that fateful Friday.

"I went immediately to the principal and told him of my mistake and begged for forgiveness. He called the police, and I was escorted to the local police department, where I waited until my mother arrived to talk to me. She was going to be so disappointed and embarrassed by my actions.

"I had let the entire family down because people were really going to think that they were horrible parents, I thought in my grief. I knew for sure that the police could do nothing to me that would be worse than what Harry was going to do to me when I got home. At the police station, I was interrogated unmercifully. *Yes, Harry,* I thought in my terror, *you were right all along. I'm a criminal idiot fag who will never amount to anything good.*

"When Mom walked through the front door of the police station, I saw the sadness and disappointment in her hazel eyes. I saw her lips quiver and her breathing deepen. Her skin was white as a ghost. I knew, reading her body language, that this was too far, and we both knew that when we arrived back home—if we got to go home, instead of being placed in prison or who knew what—Harry was going to beat the hell out of both of us for being stupid and getting caught. In a small town, any secret you want to keep, you can be sure will be spread all over town before you get home.

"I told the police the truth. You see, no matter how dysfunctional our home life, my mother would sneak (yes, sneak) around and whisper advice to me to teach my brothers (without Harry's hearing and thinking we were plotting to kill him or something) how to become better men. She told us to tell the truth even when no one would ever know. Otherwise, tell the facts despite the heartache.

"So I did exactly what Mom had taught me and made it clear to the police that I was a letdown not only to myself but to others. We were all three placed on probation for one year. This was more than embarrassing to me. My dream to be a funeral director, wear a suit and tie, and be someone my mom and dad would be proud of had just gone up in smoke because of my horrible actions. I had probation the entire year and learned many valuable lessons.

"I was expelled from school for what the principal called 'your thievery' and had to go to Challenger, a special school for unruly, unmanageable, angry, violent kids. I was so disappointed in myself. I would do my work each day, always thinking about who I was and what I had done. I sat in this large room with fifteen to twenty other students who were in there for fighting, cussing, stealing, vandalism, and violent outbursts and assaults. *This is not where I belong*, I thought with deep regret to myself. To this day, I carry the shame of my actions back then.

I wrote Oprah a letter after the incident.

Dear Oprah,

Have you ever done something you was sorry for? Did you ever take something that did not belong to you even if you was just borrowing it? Did people forgive you or hold it against you forever? I know you will know the answer to all these questions, and I will go to the mailbox morning and night till I hear from you.

PS: I promise I will always be your fan no matter what bad thing I done.

Sincerely,
James, your friend and fan in Tumbleweed, Texas

When telling Weezie my story, I always stopped after paraphrasing the Oprah letter. Because it would have upset her too much at the end of her life, I stopped telling her I overheard two teachers talking outside a Challenger classroom one afternoon near the end of school that year about my classmates and me. Prior to her last sickness, I would tell her what I heard like this: "'Alice, we are just deluding ourselves to think we can educate the masses. The sooner we come to grips with the fact that some of these children are what we call throwaway kids, the easier our job will be. My personal goal is to keep them safe from themselves and others, as far as that's possible. My sanity (and my husband's) requires that I just stop trying to do more.

"'Look at some of these kids in detention—Larry, for instance. Both sides of his family have married or had sex with their relatives. Both sides of his family have aunts, uncles, cousins, parents, and grandparents with rap sheets a mile long. Many of all these kids' parents and relatives for generations have been drug dealers, alcoholics, drug addicts, and prostitutes.

"'Many have insufficient nutrition at home to stay awake and function an entire day. Sarah's mother came to school one day last week carrying her tiny new baby brother with his bottle full of red Kool-Aid!

"'I have fought since the beginning of school to rid the school of lice. As soon as one or two kids are cured, I walk through the aisles and literally see the lice jumping across the aisle back onto the cured kids. My husband is getting so angry with me. I've drained our bank account buying Rid for those who can't afford it.

"'Some of the things these kids have seen, heard, and experienced you and I didn't even know existed until long after we were grown. Those who come to school every day with visible injuries that could not have happened the way they report they happened, leave us teachers helpless to do anything about it.'

"Alice agreed, saying, 'I know. I asked James the other day if anything bad was happening at home, and I know that he lied to me. Day after day he comes to school with black eyes, bruised limbs, or swollen lips. The principal says unless the child or an eyewitness reports abuse, there is nothing we can legally do. Who are we kidding when we think we can educate these kids with the families and environments they come from? It's just not going to happen.'

"I lowered my head in shame, resting my head on my hands in shocked recognition. I knew when they were talking about Larry that Larry's story was also mine. In that one moment, I decided I was not going to be a throwaway kid. This detention was going to be the last one for me. The term *throwaway kid* haunts me to this day.

Throwaway Kid

T hrowaway kid with no one to care,
H oping someday that he will belong,
R ejecting that God is really there.
O n borrowed time—he does not have long,
W ondering why he was even born,
A live through no choice of his own,
W ondering if he will always mourn,
A sking to be loved before he's grown,
Y earning for mentors to stand beside,
K nowing an angel will soon provide,
I nvolved in life as part of a team,
D reams coming true—newfound self-esteem.

Once when I was ending this story before she got sick, Gramma Weezie said, "I wish someone like you, Jamesy, had thrown me away and then adopted me when I was a child." My heart broke to hear her say those words.

As much as she loved the saxophone story, her favorite story by far was one we called "Beer Bandits," and that had to be followed by one she called "Pinkie." I would ham it up telling her these stories, and if I changed anything, she would instantly correct me. Just like a child, she wanted me to tell it exactly the same way every time.

I would start off each time by saying, "Now, Weezie, I'm not old enough yet for this story to get out, so promise me on your life you will never tell anyone what I did back when I was young and gullible and foolish." She would promise me faithfully that my story was safe with her, and then I would proceed.

"All my early years I had hated alcohol. I hated the way it smelled, the hold it had over Harry, and what it had done to my mother. I never once tried even a taste while living at home. To my sensitive sense of smell, its smell was vile."

Gramma Weezie knew my mom and Harry, and she would always agree because she was deathly afraid of Harry. She hated for him to come to our house for even a short period of time because of the way he treated and talked to my mom.

We would talk about that for a while, then I would continue. "In fact, when Harry would walk off with some left in a bottle on the table beside his chair, I would quickly pour it out and then run and hide. At the time I felt in my innocence that that was some control I could have over his drinking."

Weezie would then say, "You were a good boy, pouring out that stuff."

"Not all of my actions were innocent," I would admit. "I became almost obsessed with ridding the world of the nasty-smelling stuff that I held completely responsible for all of my physical wounds and psychological woes. Even today, I still catch myself blaming an inanimate liquid in a bottle for everything bad that has ever happened to me.

"Blake, my escort and cohort for this exciting adventure, had always been in Special Education when he wasn't in and out of school detention, school lockup, suspension for two or three days, and finally expulsion on many occasions. Blake hated special education and was probably trying to get expelled. He hated school and always had.

"Harry held a serious grudge and hated Blake as far back as I can remember, but I never really knew why. He spent an inordinate amount of energy keeping us boys away from him and him away from us.

"Blake years later told me he saw how my body was always bruised, how the Jock Pack would make a big deal of taunting me, even carrying a bottle of rubbing alcohol and wiping their desk and mine down with it to prevent getting AIDS from me.

"When family would say my eyes were just like my mom's,

Blake said his mama said my mama and me had the same exact sad eyes. He felt compelled to help me feel better, and beer was his cure of choice for all the woes of mankind.

"Blake affectionately called me Bro or Li'l Bro. For years he had tried to coax me into sneaking out of my bedroom window after what I called my nightly protection patrol, making sure my mom and brothers were safe and asleep, and joining him in his juvenile delinquency. Blake had been drinking since he was about nine, and knowing my hatred of being called a sissy, he told me that only sissies hated beer.

"One night as I was wheeling the trashcan out for the next early-morning trash pickup, Blake was hiding behind a bush on his bicycle. He motioned to me and coaxed me into sneaking out that night. He pointed out that he had already taken the screen off my window and had propped it up safely against the house.

"I went into the house and opened my window while everyone was still awake. Our house had two bedrooms, one bath, and no insulation, so noises were impossible to mask.

"Finally convinced that tonight was the night, I took out some clothes from a black garbage sack full of hand-me-downs from the Love Center and carefully constructed the shape of my body, covering the lump completely with my sheet and blanket.

"I stealthily stepped out of the window while my heart was beating out of my chest. I put the screen back on the window just as quietly and carefully and ran as fast as I could around the corner where Blake was waiting, albeit not so patiently.

"'Man, what took you so long? We could have robbed a bank during the time I've been waiting for you. Jump on quick, the place is about to close.' He reached in a saddlebag and handed me a beer. As we were riding along, I would pretend to take a sip, but I was actually pouring it slowly in a stream behind the bicycle, trying not to gag at the stomach-turning taste and smell.

"Our thrilling adventure had begun. Blake pumped on the bicycle pedals as hard as he could, mostly standing, and moaning as he pumped. I had no idea where we were going or what we were about to do, but at that moment, just like that Friday back in the sixth grade when my cousin helped me take the saxophone from the band hall, my life was totally in Blake's hands because I was trusting him not to harm me and keep me safe.

"We soon arrived at an old beer joint outside of town called Mama's Heartbreak. Blake bragged that he had not had to buy a beer in months. The parking lot was full of every kind of pickup known to man. Blake had learned that most of the pickups had iced-down ice chests in the back to be used after closing time for after parties at the lake. For months he had been going to the beer joint and getting one or two beers out of each truck until the basket on his bike was full.

"This particular night, Blake sneaked over to a pickup in the parking lot on the back side of the bar, leaving me behind with the instructions to watch carefully for exiting customers, warning him with my own distinctive bird-call type whistle Mr. Lay had made for me, if I spotted one.

"That night, after his saddlebags were full, Blake had what he called one of the best ideas he had ever had. He explained that we should take lots of beers, breaking them over any hard object we could find. Assured after a few minutes that no one was leaving the place, he pulled out a large empty tow sack, told me to hold it open as he emptied a couple of ice chests, and proceeded to jump in and out of the beds of the pickups.

"Blake was a large, unkempt kind of guy, with his belly hanging out in front and his butt crack exposed in the back, even before that was fashionable. When the bag got too heavy for me to carry, we would both drag it and disappear into a wooded area right behind the beer joint.

"Blake was wearing heavy steel-toed work boots, a red plaid shirt, and blue jeans that were at least a size too small. I watched with glee as he stomped one full beer can after another, spewing the liquid everywhere. The bottles were broken one after another against a large tree.

"Very soon, customers began to exit the bar in large groups. Could it already be closing time? We jumped on the bike and raced away with as much speed as we could with his bicycle heavily laden with beer. As we arrived safely back at my house, Blake insisted we have a beer together and relive our thrilling escapades of the evening.

"After only one gross touch of my tongue to the urine-colored liquid, I had to bravely admit that I did not like beer. Blake looked at me incredulously, saw I was shaking and almost in tears at my revelation, and said, 'Don't worry, Li'l Bro. I'm just sorry we didn't find no wine coolers tonight. I know you'd like them.' I almost cried at his understanding and was so grateful and relieved that he hadn't cursed me out, hit me, or worse.

"That was the first of several such escapades in the following months. We almost got caught one night. We passed a dark-skinned customer in dark clothes and black cowboy hat who stood in the dark, throwing up behind his black pickup on our way to the woods. The guy cursed at us loudly and started chasing us, and we were just glad he was too drunk to outrun us.

"After almost getting caught, we were scared straight for several weeks, thanking our lucky stars we had not gotten caught. During those weeks, Blake started stealing cigarettes for me, and I started smoking as our boredom increased. In the local paper, articles appeared warning people not to leave beer in the back of their pickups but to lock their ice chests in their cabs. We were called Beer Bandits in the headlines of the articles. We were famous, but no one but us knew it!

"I'm not sure I would have gone along with stealing the beer after that first night, hating both the smell and taste of beer, but I truly loved the idea of smashing them. The tree trunks became Harry's face to me. In my naïve thirteen-year-old mind, I justified our actions, stating three reasons to Blake.

"First, if we could smash enough of the beers, there would be a limited supply for Harry and all the other drunks to buy. Second, we could lessen the possibility that the exiting revelers at closing time would smash into innocent drivers on the road and kill somebody on their way home. And third, always in the forefront of my mind were the wives and kids at home waiting to be cursed and beaten by a drunken father returning from a night out.

"To me, it was simple math. Less beer in the world equaled less violence perpetrated on innocent victims."

Until the end of her life, Weezie always heartily agreed with me.

CHAPTER 20

RECIPE OF HAPPINESS

lways following the story of the "Beer Bandits," was one Gramma Weezie called, "Pinkie." I could never tell the Beer Bandits story without following it with the story about Pinkie. I would start the story the same way each time.

Blake and I could hardly wait for Friday and Saturday nights to come around each week. We had become addicted to stomping those beer cans and smashing those beer bottles against a tree. One by one, we were determined to rid the world of that nasty-smelling, vile-tasting liquid poison.

One Saturday night became a point of deliverance in my life. As we rounded the corner on Blake's bicycle, there was a police car parked in front and one in back of Mama's Heartbreak. Blake wheeled his bike around so tightly and quickly that he slung me off the back of the bike into a ditch. I wasn't badly hurt, but I was furious with him.

"Fuck it, Bro!" he screamed at me. "I'd rather you be mad at me out here than in a police station somewhere. Now get ahold o' yourself! The day will come when you'll be thanking me. Trust me when I tell you that tonight will change your life! I done figgered out what we can do to have some fun if you'll just shut up and listen to me.

"There's a revival tent meetin' down on the vacant lot of the fairgrounds. Let's go laugh at us some holy rollers!"

I had no idea what he was talking about. He might as well have been speaking a foreign language. I did not know what a revival tent meetin' or a holy roller was, but I was not about to reveal my ignorance to him. I told Blake I had always wanted to go to one of those and jumped excitedly onto the back of the bike, and he, none the wiser, headed out.

We had only gone a few blocks toward the fairgrounds when we heard shouting and loud music. My mounting excitement replaced my anger at Blake. I could not wait to get there and see what was happening. The tent cover was tied to ropes anchored in the ground on stakes about the height of two school rulers off the ground. We got off near the front of the tent, lay on our bellies, and peeked inside the tent.

There was not one white face in the crowd. Sitting on the front row of the gathering was our neighbor's maid, Pinkie, whom I loved with all my heart. Both by her words of wisdom and her loving example alone, she had been an important spiritual mentor to me. Pinkie's boss, Mrs. Bledsoe, our neighbor in the next block, still lived in the house where she was born.

A black now white-haired lady, Pinkie had wet-nursed Mrs. Bledsoe when she was born. Pinkie had two kids by the time she was fourteen, and Mrs. Bledsoe's mother hired her to nurse her newborn before her milk dried up, while also helping with the housework.

"Miz Bledsoe was hard to wean, oowee!" she told me often. "Finally, I'd fix that hollering baby a sugar tit. I fooled her into sucking on it so I could get the housework done. She was the most beautiful blue-eyed, blond-haired baby you ever seen, but lawzy mercy, did she have a mind of her own. Nearly drove me crazy grabbing at my breasts, unbuttoning my blouse. Mercy! Best day of my life was when I learnt she loved sugar. Yep, she still loves sugar to this day."

A sugar tit, I learned years later, was made by putting a lump of sugar in a cheesecloth type rag, twisting it up, tying a string around it to make a tit, and giving it to a toddler to suck on. (No wonder so many people had dentures so early back then!)

After Pinkie's children were grown, Pinkie had moved into the Bledsoe house permanently and nursed Mrs. Bledsoe's elderly parents until each died at home. She was now a lifelong companion to Mrs. Bledsoe.

Pinkie planted a garden each year and kept the house and yard in beautiful condition. From time to time I would sneak out and sit on the porch with Pinkie while she told me stories of her childhood and her parents' childhood. To me the stories were profoundly sad, but there was always a perceptible note of happiness in Pinky's voice when telling me the stories.

"We was pore, but we was taught to be thankful," she would tell me. "My mama taught us kids that gratitude was what made you happy. Lasting happy don't come from the outside.

"Lasting happy don't come from no bottle or no pill, no man, or no woman. No sir. Lasting happy comes from the inside, Baby Boy." (That's the name she always called me). "My mama taught us kids what her mama taught her and her brothers and sisters to say from the time we was all little: they can beat you on the outside till you bleed, but they can't beat you down inside—'less you agreed!"

There was a visiting black minister conducting the service at the revival that night. Black choir members in red robes continually and alternately stood up and sat down from a row of folding chairs while clapping and singing. The music was amazing. I thought I knew what happy looked like, but I didn't know anyone could be as happy as those folks were that night.

There is no way I can remember all that was said, but I will never forget what happened to me while listening to the service. First, in that one night my life was changed forever, just not in the way Blake had expected.

The feeling of relief that swept over me was amazing when the minister started preaching. "Now go on, brothers and sisters, if you think you can do better than God at getting back at those who use and abuse you. You just go on ahead. You know what I'm talking 'bout! I'm talking 'bout hating yo enemies."

"That's right, go on," the crowd shouted.

"On the other hand, if you think the God who made the whole world—the sun, the moon, and the stars—can do a better job of punishing your enemies, then let *him* do it." The crowd responded in loud agreement.

"Can *he* do a better job than you can?" There was a moment of silence when he said, "Help me now—somebody—please say *amen!*" The congregation in unison said a loud *amen* as they clapped and danced and sang to the music.

"Brothers and sisters, are you with me?" he shouted between stanzas as the choir hummed.

The crowd shouted back, "Yes, we're here!"

"You been beaten on the outside?"

"Yes, we have!"

"Bloodied and bruised, uh huh?"

"Yes, bloodied and bruised."

"But you happy on the inside?"

"Yes, we are!"

"Are you rejoicing 'bout it?"

"Yes we are!"

"Do you love the Lord?"

"Yes, we love you, Lord."

"Do you love your brothers?"

"Yes, we do!"

"Do you love your sisters?"

"Yes, we do!"

"Are you praying for your enemies?"

"Yes, we are!"

"Are you praying without ceasing?"

"Oh, yes, we are!"

"What about giving thanks in all circumstances?"

"Yes, pastor, we giving thanks! Thank you, Lord."

"Has God been working all things for your good?"

"Yes, Pastor, yes, he has!"

"Well then, stand up on your feet and praise God like you means it!"

The praising and rejoicing I heard that night was something I had never heard before. It took me years to express what I learned that night from those dear saints, but I already knew on some level as a teenager that, as humans, the depth of our adversity determines the capacity to which we can fully experience (and are able to express) earthly joy.

How strange—their gratitude had become the source of their unspeakable joy and happiness! I could not help but think back to the times Mom played Igor with us and when she would play dead for us.

The horrible things we'd just experienced a short time before suddenly disappeared, and we immediately were filled with joy, jumping around and shouting just like those saints on a hot, sultry Texas night under a tent, under the stars.

"Weezie, as sure as you and I are both sitting here, I was convinced that the Big God used Blake that night to teach me to give to God the shackles tying the hate around my heart and let him take care of Harry however he saw fit—and in his time, not mine."

"I believe that, too, Jamesy," Weezie would say.

I waited a moment and then continued. "Blake thought I was still angry with him for pitching me in the ditch because of my silence on our way home, but in my silence I was ignoring Blake's mocking of a moving service and a grateful crowd as I was thanking the Big God for setting me free from my anger, hatred, and all-consuming thirst for vengeance.

"Weezie, I been thinking about it. Do you think Blake was being so hateful that night 'cause he's just had it too easy? Could it be he hadn't had enough suffering to be able to know what joy and happiness look and feel like?"

"Maybe, Jamesy. But I really think he just never learned to be thankful."

"You know what?" I responded. "I think we're both right."

The next time I saw Pinky, she was pulling weeds in the driveway. Wildflowers were growing up between the cracks in the buckled-up concrete. "Come here, Baby Boy," she called to me as I waved to her. "See these beautiful yellow wildflowers?

"Now God outdid hisself on this one," she said as she tenderly picked a flower. "See how perfect it is? See the beautiful rich color? This perfect little flower was growing in rocks and gravel.

"I don't see no rich topsoil nowhere near it. Didn't nobody plant it but God. Didn't nobody water it but God. Didn't nobody give it sunshine but God. Didn't nobody but God protect it from the harsh spring winds and rain.

"That's just like you and me, Baby Boy. Don't you never tell nobody I said this, but I think we's both beautiful, perfect wildflowers growing in the rocks and gravel on this earth. One perfect black flower and one perfect white one. Didn't nobody plant us here but God. Didn't nobody water or feed us but God. Didn't nobody but God put that sun up in the sky to shine down on us.

"Just look at us! Lawzy mercy, ain't we beautiful?" Pinkie's sweet laugh filled my eyes with tears. "There's no doubt in my mind," she continued, "that God *knows* he outdid hisself on both of us! No doubt indeed.

"Now you get on home, Baby Boy, and help yo sweet mama, ya hear?"

Pinkie's Recipe for Happiness
Bloom where you are planted,
Take nothing for granted.

As God supplies each need,
Give thanks in word and deed.

Dear Oprah:

After being at a revival tent meeting the other night, I saw how hard it is for anyone to be a Christian. They love the Ten Commandments and that's fine (most of them), but they have some that are impossible to keep, like rejoice always. How in the world can a person rejoice when somebody has beaten them up calling them a sissy or cussing them out? They have another command to pray without ceasing. How can you pray even when you're sleeping or trying to figure out a math problem? I can only do one at a time. Another one is to give thanks in all situations. Now that's the most impossible one right there. My neighbor Pinkie says to give thanks 'cause God has something better for you right around the corner where you can't see it. If that's true I wish the command would just go ahead and say to give thanks in all circumstances because the circumstances just might be setting you up for something better, but that isn't what it says. What do you think? I hope you will answer my letter and tell me what you think cause you are always happy or mainly how you do it. Oh well. Thinking too hard makes me sleepy so I'll try to stop worrying and go on to sleep and do my best to keep the Ten Commandments. That's already one too many for me anyways.

Sincerely,
James, your friend and fan in Tumbleweed, Texas

My current spiritual mentor is my beloved Beth Cohen, who reminds us often through the story of Ruth in the Torah to give of our best to the poor. Just as Ruth never blamed God for the premature death of her first husband—a devastating blow to her as a young woman—neither should we today blame God for our losses.

Because of Ruth's faithfulness, and in spite of her tragic loss early in her life, she became the ancestor of the great King David and his son, King Solomon, who was reportedly the wisest man to ever live.

If Joseph could forgive his brothers for selling him into slavery and leave all vengeance to God, so can we, Rabbi Cohen points out.

She helps me to continue to forgive Harry, not for him but for me. She has taught me to thank God for the way He has used all my abuse and losses and worked them for my good, just as he had done in Ruth and Joseph's life. How indebted I know that I am. And because of all that's been done for me, I am a very grateful Jew.

On waves of suffering, pain, and loss,
Countless gifts and angels reach life's shore,
Treasures unveiled by the ebbing tide
Sent to avenge, renew, and restore.

Isaiah 61:3 says God will provide:
"a crown of beauty instead of ashes,
the oil of gladness instead of mourning,
and a garment of praise
instead of a spirit of despair."

CHAPTER 21

BECAUSE OF YOU

Studying in closet after closet, often shut off from the outside world, slowly but surely my dream of having a higher education was getting closer and closer. Research papers were getting more and more enjoyable, and soon I knew I would at least have a Master's Degree in forensic psychology.

My physical hunger in graduate school while working on my Master's Degree with only minimal sustenance, however, was giving me more pain than when I was younger. When the class voted on a list of topics and chose the topic of hunger for an hour-long, extemporaneous pop quiz class paper, I was elated.

The teacher later commented that I was the only student in the class who started writing immediately, and my paper was by far the longest. All the other students were having a hard time with the topic. An excerpt from memory follows.

I am convinced that God gives the starving a gift of eventually not feeling hunger to some degree, or at least that was my experience. When I see pictures of starving children on television, I send a donation with a prayer that God will give them the same lack of pain I felt when I was hungry as a child.

From as early as could remember, I would sneak food from my Aunt Rosie's pantry in the middle of the night for my brothers and me. I knew what hunger felt like. I knew the gnawing craving, the gut-wrenching signals the brain sends to warn us that if we don't get food soon, we will not live another day.

One day when I was seven, I had been planning our late-night meal all day long. Mom's government check would not arrive for several more days, and desperation was moving up the ladder from being my middle name to being my first name. Hunger was my primary motivation in life, and until it was satisfied, I could think of nothing else.

I knew my brothers' favorite canned-goods meal and was praying the pantry would have canned pork and beans, tomatoes, SPAM, six slices of Wonder Bread, and Miracle Whip in the refrigerator. The last time I had looked, I thanked God Aunt Rosie was a hoarder, because she had rows of these items, lined up, just waiting for me to borrow one of each from the back of each row until the day I could pay her back.

That was one of the hottest nights I can remember, and the unrelenting Texas heat was literally taking my breath away. I remember getting out of bed and rolling around on the cooler floor, away from my brother's steaming body heat and perspiration, waiting for my mom and dad to fall asleep.

At that moment in time, I would have given any one of my precious body parts for a cool breath of air, a SPAM sandwich, and a cool drink of water. Then maybe I could live another day to see that my brothers were fed.

Finally, the house was quiet. My mom had stopped crying and telling Harry, "Please, please, stop and let me sleep." In a few short minutes, Harry's snoring could be heard above the night sounds of the whirring refrigerator motor in the kitchen and crickets outside our open windows.

When we moved into the house, the landlord told us the refrigerator did not work properly and we would have to get another one. It was a small white Frigidaire refrigerator, probably built in the '40s or '50s. The rust spots had been covered with spray paint that was now peeling off, exposing the rust once again.

The floor around the refrigerator was always sparkling clean because the refrigerator leaked and the water had to be mopped up in the morning when Mom first got up, at least once during the day and at night before she went to bed. That was the only refrigerator we had the entire time we lived there.

The altered sound of Dad's breathing signaled the arrival of REM sleep. I silently got up off the floor, tiptoed barefooted to the back door where I had earlier propped the creaking screen door open with a large rock, and left for Aunt Rosie's pantry, dressed only in my silky black, air-conditioned shorts with raveling seams.

As soon as I knew I was about to access nourishment, the pain returned with the hunger. Alarms started going off in my brain that I was on borrowed time, teetering on the brink of the starvation cliff.

The house was pitch dark except for two tiny nightlights in the walls in the kitchen and hall. The two-sided refrigerator was black, but I felt the handle in the darkness and gave it a tug. It opened a couple of inches, then made a loud noise when it hit the chain Aunt Rosie had put around the entire refrigerator, with a combination lock connecting the two ends of the chain.

I stood in the darkness a moment, holding back the tears, waiting to make sure the loud noise hadn't waked anyone up. All remained silent as I headed for the pantry door. A new knob needing a key to unlock it had been installed. Everything was locked up tight.

I ran several houses away before I screamed up at God through my sobs, "Where are you? Why do you let this happen to us? Some liar told me you were my shepherd."

The entire family was sound asleep when I got back home. I kissed my brothers and whispered to them I would find a way to feed them. Remarkably, my actual pilfering was never discovered. The irony was that what we were accused of stealing was something we had not taken.

Aunt Rosie's favorite dessert was Little Debbie's Oatmeal Creme Pies. She hid them behind cans in her pantry. She was always accusing someone of stealing them. That is something I never stole. I had never seen one before the day she made her accusation. We did not even know where she kept them until one day she accusingly showed us where a missing box had been.

Once on a rare occasion Aunt Rosie asked if we'd like to have one. We were skeptical that it was a setup. When she convinced us she wasn't kidding, she got one out, cut it in fourths, gave a fourth each to my two brothers and me, and popped the last fourth into her mouth. I had never tasted anything so delicious.

More and more of my why questions were beginning to be answered in mandatory group counseling sessions, realizing my dream of finally understanding why some of the things had been happening to me.

I was shocked to learn that no one can remain an addict without an enormous amount of help. These helpers are called codependents. Codependents love to focus on and blame the identified problem (i.e., Harry), with less focus on the unidentified problem, my mom and even me, without whom he could not remain an addict. Harry was masterful at finding multiple enablers, or plan B, as he would refer to them threateningly.

I realized my mom was just as addicted to Harry as Harry was to the alcohol, nicotine, and sex. Harry was her drug of choice. Like all addicts, Harry and Mom's addictions were more important to them than air, water, food, or the welfare of their dependent children. Addicts will sacrifice everything most people hold dear to enable other addicts and/or to satisfy their insatiable cravings.

The victims, the ones who usually get all or most of the sympathy, become addicted and willing volunteers in the vicious cycle. Only when the volunteers stop enabling will the addict hit bottom and seek help.

With the help of a skilled therapist and a group of other addicted enablers/addicts who gave truthful, painful feedback to me in a group setting, I had to eventually accept my role in enabling my mom to keep enabling Harry. When I became financially able, I had bought her all the necessities of life she was doing without. When her electricity or water was cut off, I paid the bill. Those actions enabled her to give Harry all the money she ever got to feed his addictions! I had to admit I had become addicted to enabling my mother. Addiction is a vicious and deadly family disorder.

Right out of mortuary school our dream of actually making a living in our chosen field came true. Asa and I worked for different funeral homes in the same town. We were grateful for our jobs, but we both had always talked and dreamed of owning our own business.

As a result, through the years we have refurbished two different buildings in two different towns and realized our dream. We both love the funeral business and always will. To say it is in our blood is an understatement.

We got another once-in-a-lifetime opportunity to own our own mortuary in the shadow of the medical examiner's office in downtown Austin. The education and life experiences we have been blessed with have been above and beyond our wildest dreams. We sold our funeral home, refurbished a duplex, and went into business in the black financially on the first day in our new mortuary business. We lived in one side and had the other side for the business.

When talking with the police department prior to acquiring the property about the crime in the bad neighborhood near downtown Austin, the captain assured us everything should be relatively safe there. Their experience had been that a mortuary was no-man's land to most perpetrators.

"Typically, most perpetrators leave this part of town and go to the suburbs to conduct their malfeasance," the lieutenant said with a grin on his face. "There's very little crime in or near a funeral home or mortuary. The only way it could be safer," he declared with a laugh, "would be if it were also near a cemetery."

That assessment turned out to be absolutely true. We never had a hearse vandalized or broken into, and we would smile when we'd see most of the neighbors cross to the other side of the street when nearing the property while out walking.

Owning a mortuary is a young man's business. It is not for the faint-hearted. Asa and I could never be off at the same time, and our relationship began to suffer. Night after night, week after week, tragedy was all around us. Every Monday and Tuesday we would pick up young bodies from the medical examiner's office that had been stabbed, shot, or otherwise terminally dispatched in the previous weekend's mayhem.

Mostly minority young men were being killed off at a staggering rate. We rarely knew the particulars of any case unless there was an article in the newspaper about it.

The cases that took their toll most profoundly on us were the small children—beaten, raped, choked, bones broken, many unrecognizable. Too many never even had anyone to care enough to pick up their tiny broken bodies or cremains.

Asa and I spoke when we received each case about how great it would be if we could step in and make a difference before a tag was put on another tiny child's ankle. I knew how easily I could have been a statistic as a child myself. With a touch of survivor's guilt, I would often ask myself why I had been repeatedly snatched from the trash heap and others had not.

At the same time, a dream of another nature came true. Ashira and Leah's mother remarried, and the new family unit that resulted became an intolerable situation. Out of that turmoil, though, came the ultimate blessing of the girls coming to live with us permanently.

We will always be grateful to Judge Haddock and Attorney Demi Hive for guiding us through the legal maze associated with custody disputes. Particularly on each girl's birthday and holidays, we acknowledge and express our gratitude for the role the girls' mother played in giving birth to these two amazing human beings.

As an accountant, Asa functions more in the left side of his brain, so any discussion about actually following through and adopting a child was met with resistance. He was focused on the lifelong financial and emotional commitment we would be making, so for a long time I put that dream on hold.

At the time we were fostering newborn twin girls while their mother was trying to sober up and get them back. They were taking up a lot of my love and attention. We were helping many friends and family foster and adopt as well. Every day, sometimes multiple times per day, time ran out for some child in a perilous situation, and I felt a great sense of relief when each child could be saved from a fate like mine when I was a child.

One day Asa, without any warning, came in with his usual boyish I've-got-a-secret grin. He pitched a free local parents' magazine on the kitchen counter where I was cooking dinner one night.

The ad read:

CRISIS IN TEXAS: ADOPTIVE PARENTS NEEDED IMMEDIATELY.

I immediately answered the ad and started the application process. I would not let my hopes get up, because most agencies would not allow a single, much less gay, man to adopt.

Less than a year later, we got a call to come to Ridge Hospital in Hill Country, Texas, where we picked up our four-pound, eleven-ounce newborn baby girl, Adiya. At the time same-sex couples could not adopt, so I was the adoptive parent, and Adiya has both Asa's and my last name. She was ours, and we were hers. Finally, we had an angel who resembled the pictures of angels I had seen and admired since my childhood, except one thousand times more beautiful.

After we had owned the mortuary for nearly two years, our dream of exchanging vows came true. We also badly needed a vacation. One of us had had to be on call at all times, and our relationship was beginning to suffer from the lack of time together. Our oldest daughter, Ashira, was eight years old, Leah had just turned five, and our baby, Adiya, celebrated her first birthday on the trip home.

All my life, I had helped friends plan, design, and implement their wedding arrangements, but something was missing. Asa and I wanted to make it official that he was mine and I was his. The date was set for June 16, 2007.

We had a good professional crew working for us at the mortuary, and it took us all to put the plans together while still running the mortuary. We had wonderful friends in the flower business who blew out all the stops on the flowers. We had friends in the bakery business who gave us a marvelous discount on the refreshments. We rented a home near downtown that was known for its beautiful setting for weddings.

Most of our dear friends and family came and blessed us with their presence, their gifts, their love, and their prayers for a happy, healthy, prosperous life together. There were friends and family members who had religious objections and stayed away.

Asa and I knew, for our own good, we had to accept their deeply held views and love them anyway, especially if we expected them to honor our opposite feelings, orientation, and views.

A plaque hangs in our bedroom that I wrote and gave to Asa on our day:

Alone we're content,
Together we are better,
God's amazing plan.

Spiritual love
Knows that giving is better
So often receives.

When you are empty,
I'll have plenty in reserve
From when you filled me.

When you are upset,
I will listen to your rants
Like you last heard mine.

When your body aches,
I will massage you with oil
The way you do me.

When we have losses,
We'll share what money can't buy
To soften the blow.

When one of us leaves,
Alone we will be content
Till we're both back home.

An older friend and her grandson Ashton, age thirteen, were
working with us for the summer and agreed to accompany us on
our honeymoon to help manage the three children. They both
kept the children in one room, and Asa and I had our room.
Ashton, a football player and weightlifter, carried Adiya all over
New York City, and Gran kept the children at night while I did

online schoolwork or we guys went out after the kids went to bed. We celebrated Adiya's first birthday on the plane flying home.

Ashton was the young man I had prayed about being able to mentor just like Mr. Pastore had mentored me. He spent two subsequent summers interning with me in the funeral business. We have become lifelong friends, and after his stint in the navy, I have offered him a job to come back and work for me.

My remembered dream and the promise I had made to myself many years prior that if I ever had children I would take them to Disney World was about to be fulfilled. We first flew to New York City for a week, and then we flew to Disney World for several days.

On that flight from New York to Florida, I smiled to myself when I realized that after all these years of dreaming of it, I was finally about to make it to Disney World—with my three amazing little girls!

When I stepped off the plane in Orlando and felt the oppressive June heat and humidity, however, I had to chuckle to myself, wondering if all the Christians attending didn't wonder if they were the ones already in the Other Place after all.

CHAPTER 22

TELLING MY STORY

Many people ask me what inspired me to tell my story at this point in time. First of all, I have never wavered from the determination that my story would one day be told. I just did not know how or when. One day right before finishing mortuary school and getting my associate's degree in applied science, I was beginning to have some anxiety about where to continue my education and what to study next.

I knew if I dropped out of school, I would have to start paying my student loan back if I didn't find a job within six months. I had a job lined up, but it was only a beginning salary until I proved myself and was not enough to pay rent, much less pay a large loan back. As long as I was in school, I could roll the debt forward until I could afford to start paying it back.

I was surfing online at the Jewish funeral home one day after ordering an oversized casket for a decedent who was a very large man. I was toying with the idea of pursuing a Bachelor's Degree in psychology for a couple of reasons.

First, I knew that grief counseling was desperately needed in the funeral industry. I saw counseling as fitting hand in glove with my chosen field of funeral service. I had been doing it for years unofficially, but I needed a degree to do it professionally.

For years I had seen how we in the industry would abruptly

enter into people's lives in times of great loss for only a matter of days and too many times would never see them again. A tragic exception was when they had taken their own lives because of the inability to process their loss and grief.

Second, looking back I know that at age twenty my life was still full of too many unanswered why questions that haunted me daily and badly needed to be answered. Too often I was recreating dysfunctional relationships with men who continued my childhood abuse. I would fall in love, only soon to see traumatic flashbacks of my father in my current partner's actions. Maybe, I thought, psychology would help me answer those why questions.

I took an introduction to psychology test. There were several questions I remember that were asked that I think of often to this day. The instructions were to answer them in a paragraph or two, giving detailed examples where possible to determine if psychology was the path a student both desired and was qualified to pursue.

1. Describe your early and current relationship to your mother first, then to your father.
2. Do you matter to those closest to you?
3. Do those closest to you reward or punish you for your accomplishments?
4. Do you attract destructive people into your life?
5. How do you train other people to treat you the way they do?
6. How do you respond when people break promises, let you down, or belittle you?
7. Are you willing to learn how to let others mirror your actions back to you without lashing out?
8. Are you willing to learn how to calmly, yet firmly, mirror others' behaviors back to them without fear of reprisal?
9. Describe how you respond to compliments, awards, diplomas, and accomplishments. Give specific examples.
10. Describe any lessons you have learned from your failures.

I quickly started writing answers to those questions after that mindless clicking on the Internet and could not stop. Instead of stopping at the required paragraph, I wrote pages. The pages turned into chapters.

Those chapters filled countless dog-eared notebooks that were used to help earn me a Bachelor's Degree in general psychology, a Master's Degree in forensic psychology, and finally a Ph.D in counseling psychology.

Those notebooks continue filling up shelves today as I continue to journal while finishing my first book, telling the story I started documenting as a seven-year-old child.

Dear Oprah:

In my last letter to you I want to first thank you for some specific, larger ways in which you influenced my life. First, because of your emphasis on education, I went from high–school dropout in the eleventh grade to a Ph.D., one college class at a time.

Because of seeing your love for underprivileged children all over the world, and identifying with them, I've chosen a profession in which I help find loving foster and adoptive parents for unloved children. Because of our shared suffering, I was never alone in my suffering. Your example of overcoming adversity provided proof that I too could overcome mine.

Because of your shows on suicide, you saved my life on more than one occasion by encouraging anyone in your audience who was considering suicide to stop, reach out to a trusted friend, and consider that whatever seemed hopeless would pass. You were right—it always did, and I am still here.

My story is now recorded because of your admonition that everyone should keep a daily journal.

Because of your encouragement to keep a gratitude list, my blessings were listed each day at the bottom of my journal entries. Emphasis went from my abuse and sorrows to thanking God for the simplest things.

On a lighter note, following are just a few examples of how I think of you most days of every week as I change the world around me for the better one small step at a time.

Your makeovers of impoverished women, who had lived all their lives unselfishly giving to other people, inspire me to this day. When I make small changes in hair, makeup, and choices of shoes and clothes for friends and family for special occasions, or a foster parent on court day, I silently think of you and your shows.

Applying makeup, styling hair, and dressing a cadaver those long days at the mortuary was not just a way to provide for my family in the funeral business; those small acts that you referred to as "random acts of kindness" became a lasting gift to the survivors of each deceased.

Because of your show on bringing order out of chaos in a cluttered home, I can now help potential foster parents prepare their homes for state inspection and make it that much more possible to play a part in providing a child with a loving home.

One such simple change I've often used regards organizing books on shelves in order of height and bringing them all flush with the edges of the shelves. A short ten—minute segment on one of your shows has helped me use this simple technique to change countless homes and lives for the better—on a daily basis. I can't tell you how many waiting rooms I've surreptitiously transformed in this way while waiting for an appointment.

By buying matching frames (often at a dollar store when money is tight), as an expert advised on one of your shows, I'm able to make a wall grouping of pictures look like an interior designer has just left a modest home. Now a loving and giving home not only looks great but also is ready to provide an ordered environment for a child whose life has been defined by chaos. Changing the world in small ways for the better—one bookshelf, one wall grouping, one home, one parent, one child, and even one dead person at a time—gives me the satisfaction that a paycheck, no matter how large, could ever match. This is all thanks to your show.

If you multiply the gifts you gave me by the millions of fans whose lives you have touched in too many ways to list, you can begin to understand the breadth of your influence. It is with a grateful heart I owe you a debt I can only begin to repay by paying it forward.

For all you are and all you do,
This grateful fan thanks God for you.
James W. Mercer, Ph.D.

There is no greater agony than bearing
an untold story inside you.
—Maya Angelou

CHAPTER 1

MOMENTS OF SHEER TERROR

"Grab a body suit, Ashton, and step into it to cover your clothes. We've been called to an unattended death on Sparks Street," James, the owner of Mercer Funeral Home, told his trusted fourteen-year-old helper. "The neighbors have reported an odor coming from the house at 777, so grab us a couple of the heavy-duty masks and head to the hearse. Clean out anything left in the back from the last call, and steel yourself for most likely the worst thing you have ever seen."

Visibly undaunted, Ashton obeyed orders.

James had learned from his mentor, Mr. Pastore, back home in his youth that a young man wanted and needed a job, not a handout. Mr. Pastore had changed James's life forever when he had given him a job almost twenty years before, and now James was helping a young man with a single mom and a younger brother, badly in need of extra income. James had more than an idea of how much this job meant to Ashton and his family, and he loved teaching Ashton about the funeral business.

More than that, though, he was fulfilling a promise he had made to himself years ago that he would do his best to be a good man like Mr. Pastore. He was committed to giving back by mentoring unemployed young men the way he had been mentored in his youth.

Ashton was a handsome, strapping young man with a ripped body from weight lifting at school. He had several trophies that documented his achievements. He had a blue-black beard he had shaved twice a day since age eleven, dark brown, almost black eyes, and a sports-type buzzed-off haircut his grandmother gave him twice a month. The first time she reluctantly buzzed off his hair before his first "two a days" in the seventh grade, his nanny sadly swept the shiny black curls on the floor into the dustpan before putting them into the garbage can. In grade school Ashton had been teased about his curls and kept his sports haircut year round to avoid the unwelcome attention. He played football in junior high and was the size of a grown man.

The first random act of kindness James performed for Ashton was buying him a new pair of the finest athletic shoes, explaining that a good, supportive pair of shoes was necessary for the job. In fact, he explained, aware of a young man's pride, that it was a safety issue and something the company had to furnish. James never mentioned the flopping sole on Ashton's left shoe that he hid behind the opposing knee during the hiring interview.

People often mistook Ashton for a college student. This summer he was doing odd jobs around the funeral home, buying food and necessities for his single mom and brother with each paycheck. He kept asking James to give him more hours and responsibility, but James was deliberately reminding himself of just how very young Ashton was. He was taking it slowly, fully aware of how disturbing some of the calls could be.

As they arrived at the reported residence, they had to park in front of the neighbor's house because a police car, an ambulance, a fire truck, and a late-model Honda filled up all the space in front of the tiny, rundown shack. James recognized the Honda as the same one that belonged to his friend, the justice of the peace everyone called "Judge."

James was beginning to have second thoughts about taking Ashton with him on this call and decided he would give him a chance to back out. The grass, mostly weeds, was grown up in the yard with a couple of weeks' worth of newspapers scattered both on and off the porch. A rusty old lawnmower was propped up against the peeling paint on the old house.

The stench of death (an indescribable odor that never leaves you once you have encountered it) attacked their noses, lungs, eyes, and mouths as they stepped onto the yard. An old 1982 rusted-out Chevy pickup truck sat in the driveway with two flat tires. All external clues James was assessing pointed to the fact that this call was probably going to be much worse than he had first imagined.

As James pitched a mask from his left hand to Ashton and put the one in his right hand on his face, the first responders inside the house exited, coughing and gagging. The usually gregarious and humorous Judge was gasping for what sounded like his last breath. The gurney, with a large heavy black plastic bag strapped on top, was unloaded from the back of the hearse as James and Ashton rushed toward the house. Ashton's heart was beating out of his chest, but his calm exterior was that of a man twice his age and experience. James thought back on his first death call, and Ashton reminded him a lot of himself at thirteen years old.

The policemen started cordoning off the perimeter of the house with crime scene tape and ordered several nosy rowdy, opinionated, talkative, and arguing neighbors from the premises. As James and Ashton stepped onto the creaking front porch, James turned to Ashton and said, "Bud, you don't have to go in if you don't want to. Just say so, and I'll get the policemen and ambulance drivers to help me with the removal."

"Not on your life; I'm going to do what I have to do," Ashton surprisingly heard himself say, bravely suppressing his gut feeling to bolt and run.

As their eyes adjusted to the light upon entering the house, they heard TNT playing loudly on a large-screen TV in the den past the living room in this shotgun-style older home, probably built before WWII. As they entered the den, they first saw what appeared to be an enormous older man sitting in a recliner with a watery liquid dripping off the seat onto the floor.

Firmly grasped in the man's hands were a TV Guide and a

remote. He looked like he had been pumped up with a bicycle pump. His skin was so thin that all the veins were showing through his translucent flesh. He sat halfway reclining, eyes totally sunk in, facing straight ahead toward the TV screen. The squirming maggots were obviously mechanically programmed by some invisible source to destroy what was left of his face.

James pointed Ashton to the left side of the chair as he headed for the right side, pulling the gurney up beside the chair. As Ashton reached the other side of the chair, he grasped his mouth with his left hand, suppressing an audible response. Lying below and in front of him was what remained of a dog, teeming with maggots, loyally lying on the floor beside his master's recliner.

Ashton had always been an avid animal lover. Reflecting back on this moment hours later as he and James debriefed on the experience, he mused that he had been so touched by the loyalty of this animal and knew in his heart that this treasured companion had truly been the alone and lonely decedent's best friend.

Without a word, James nodded for Ashton to lower the legs of the recliner gently. As he did as ordered, the body's left foot exploded all over the room and covered them, the TV, and surrounding furniture with watery, putrid-smelling liquid. The deceased's brown moccasin, full of flesh and liquid, flying almost in slow motion, stuck to the TV screen before falling to the floor with an audible thump.

Stunned, they quickly looked up and back realizing the body was slowly moving forward as the body detached from the skin that was staying glued to the chair.

The body burst, and fluid gushed like a waterfall onto the floor. The body deflated like a punctured balloon and was too fragile to pick up. Ashton felt sincere gratitude for the person or persons who had designed and made the mask he was wearing. If the odor were any worse without the mask, he was sure he would have at the very least have gagged and vomited, or most likely would have passed out cold.

James went into overdrive and automatically put the specially designed plastic bag over the body's head, seamlessly slipping it under the buttocks, forcing it down the legs, sticking the exposed bone of the left foot into the bag, and zipping up the bottom zipper. Ashton assisted as if he'd done this job all his life. They both, with all the strength each could muster, lifted the surprisingly heavy bag onto the gurney. James was flabbergasted at Ashton's seemingly superhuman strength. From each side, after momentarily catching their breath, they strapped the bag safely to the gurney.

Ashton hesitated a moment, knowing if the body had been one of his beloved parents or grandparents, also all animal lovers, that he would have wanted the remains of the decomposing animal put in the bag with the decomposing body. The thought remained a thought since he knew he was just a follower and not the leader of this operation.

With one sad glance back at the remains of the decomposing animal, pulling each leg straight up and straight down, as in a military march to avoid slipping in the fluid, Ashton and James with white knuckles pushing and tightly grasping the gurney to keep their torsos from falling, headed for the door that seemed literally miles away.

After putting the gurney back in the hearse, reassured that the attending responders had completed the investigation and all the required paperwork, they sped away quickly, heading straight for the medical examiner's office, an hour and a half away. Any unattended death in Texas requires a trip to the medical examiner's office to determine if an autopsy is needed.

Ashton sat quietly in the passenger's seat reflecting on something his coach had told his team many times. "You will most likely not soon know what all your athletic training is preparing you to do in your life. It may be years before you realize this, but trust me when I tell you that all this struggle you are going through (training in the heat, varying degrees of painful injuries, pushing yourself past anything you think you can do, being deprived of fluids, and wishing you had never started this in the first place) is not just about, and will not end, with weight lifting and football games."

Ashton thought to himself that he could not wait for school to start so he could go by and tell his coach about his summer job that had allowed him to experience this profound truth in only months, not years.

While driving along, James remembered Mr. Pastore's kindness when a mourner would ruin a freshly tailored suit with tears mixed with makeup or the many times his ruined shoes had been replaced by his kind boss without a word.

Instinctively, without Ashton's saying a word, James assured him that the athletic shoes he had bought him when he had started the job would be replaced and never mentioned again. The odor would be impossible to remove with soap, water, or chemicals no matter what claims were written on the bottle.

Ashton felt tears rushing to his eyes over his new boss's profound kindness. He thought to himself that he wanted to be a good man like this boss when he grew up.

In towns and cities all over Texas, professional, retired, temporarily unemployed, or underemployed men meet each morning starting at dawn in a coffee shop to "solve all the world's problems" while giving their wives a break from fixing breakfast. Many such establishments have a board with hangers for each participant's own ceramic coffee mug brought from home to save paper.

Payment for the coffee is typically on the honor system, and each patron serves himself from the bottomless commercial pot of steaming hot coffee. This morning ritual commonly involves going over any articles in the newspaper, where the participants often argue their differing points of view as if trying to convince an invisible jury that their view is correct.

Many night workers head for the coffee shop before going home to sleep all day before starting again all over the next evening. Many wives, female friends, and-or daughters jokingly refer to these gatherings as male-bonding sessions and to the participants as "podna boys," clueless about the men's attraction to and enjoyment of the activity.

James, several days later, went to the coffee shop at 6:00 a.m. after working most of the night embalming a family of six hit by an eighteen-wheeler driver who went to sleep at the wheel, crossed the median, and hit the family's vehicle head on. James would often drop by after a long, difficult night to decompress before heading home for a nap. This morning his friend Judge, pointing to an empty chair beside him, silently motioned for him to come sit by him.

Quietly and sadly, Judge confidentially whispered to James that he had learned while completing the extensive paperwork required on every case that the decedent on Sparks Street, where they had met several days earlier, had a son who lived three streets away from the decedent's house but had never gone by to visit or check on his dad.

Printed in the United States
By Bookmasters